Protecting Networks with SATAN

Protecting Networks with SATAN

Martin Freiss

translated by Robert Bach

Beijing · Cambridge · Köln · Paris · Sebastopol · Taipei · Tokyo

Protecting Networks with SATAN
by Martin Freiss
Translated by Robert Bach

Published by O'Reilly & Associates, Inc., 101 Morris Street, Sebastopol, CA 95472.

Editor: Elke Hansel

English Language Editor: Gigi Estabrook

Production Editor: Clairemarie Fisher O'Leary

Printing History:

August 1997:	First Edition.
May 1998:	First English Edition.

ISBN: 1-56592-425-8   [9/98]

Table of Contents

Foreword

End of Internet predicted.[*]

As the release date of SATAN came near in April 1995, the hype in the media reached bizarre proportions. Writing and releasing SATAN was a learning experience for everyone involved. One of the lessons that I learned: free publicity is great but you cannot control what they say about you.

The evolution of the Internet proceeds with leaps and bounds. This is especially true for Internet security. In the dark ages before 1988, there was hardly any practical literature about setting up systems securely. At the same time, it was difficult to obtain any information at all about security flaws; such matters were not discussed in the open. Security was a matter of obscurity, and the existence of security flaws was swept under the carpet.

This situation changed dramatically in November 1988, when Robert Tappan Morris lost control of a program that automatically broke into computer systems through the Internet. The program exploited known weaknesses in networking software and trust relations between systems. This "Internet worm" program was so successful that large portions of the Internet ceased functioning, either because machines crashed due to overload, or because system administrators disconnected their networks from the Internet. Confusion reigned for several days.

Several lessons were learned from this episode. One crucial insight was that vulnerabilities were no longer problems of individual machines. The worm demonstrated that a single security hole can make many thousands of machines vulnerable

---

[*] Since its inception, at least once a year the media has predicted the death of the Internet, whether because of the enormous growth in the volume of traffic, the release of programs like SATAN, or the contents of some web servers. And what has the Internet done? It has continued to grow and flourish.

at the same time—and since then the Internet has grown by more than a factor of 100. The existence of security flaws is no longer swept under the carpet—nowadays, vendors produce security patches in response to vulnerabilities found in their software, and security teams send out bulletins to mailing lists and newsgroups to announce the availability of these patches.

Since the days of the Internet worm, many books and articles have been written about setting up systems and networks securely, and many security tools have become available to aid in this process. All this did not make the Internet secure. Despite the availability of security literature, security tools, and security patches, many systems were connected to the network in a very insecure state. Obviously, there was a lack of awareness of the existence of security problems.

If the Internet worm broke a taboo, that of discussing the existence of vulnerabilities, SATAN broke another taboo, that of pointing out vulnerable systems on a network. Two years later, scanning the local network for bad hosts has become standard practice in many places, and SATAN has been recognized as a tool to improve network security.

In this handy book, Martin Freiss explains the workings of SATAN and provides a helping hand with customizing and extending the system to match local conditions. The author has the insight that, for many readers, SATAN scanning can be the beginning of a systematic approach to network security. Therefore, the book goes beyond SATAN and discusses basic network security techniques, gives guidance in setting up a security policy, and provides pointers to other resources that deal with the security of systems.

—Wietse Venema, SATAN co-author

Preface

Internet and Security

With phrases like information highway, web surfing, and home page, the Internet has gained immense momentum in recent months and years. While participation in the Internet was originally restricted to specialists in the computer industry and at universities, thanks to the widespread acceptance of the World Wide Web (WWW), this global network has developed into a medium for everyone.

More and more commercial organizations and private persons are connecting their computers to the Internet. The number of people involved in data exchange on the Internet is currently estimated at 50 million, and the growth rate is exponential, with the number of users about doubling every year.

Due to the rate at which the Internet, especially email and the World Wide Web, is advancing into private households and companies, the Internet is becoming more interesting as a medium for advertising and sales. Recently, commercial offerings on the World Wide Web have increased dramatically. More and more, companies are offering their products and services via electronic channels. In addition to a simple presence on the Web with advertising pages, many companies allow online ordering. New kinds of offerings are developing constantly. The development of secure payment systems for the Internet (buzzword: *electronic cash*) will further stimulate the commercialization of the Internet and encourage the growth of the spectrum of available services.

These developments are also radically changing the security requirements of the networked organizations. Previously, anyone connected to the Internet was among friends, and the Internet, although important, was not mission-critical. In those few cases where intrusion took place, damage could be controlled.

Nowadays, by contrast, the former Internet playground has become serious business—companies and universities depend on the Internet for communication. For companies that handle customer orders or that provide online services such as database research, business success depends directly on their Internet connection functioning properly. However, in connecting a system or a network to the Internet a company also bears the consequence that all Internet users thereby receive more or less unrestricted access to the company's system. If a company's services are to be utilized by customers, that company's systems must be at least partially accessible. This is accompanied by the danger of attempted intrusion from the outside into the networked host. As the Internet grows and gains economic importance, the potential danger of unwanted activities grows with it.

In large companies, the damage that could be inflicted by a malevolent intruder is enormous and beyond easy quantification. Not only can crippling the Internet connection itself inflict high costs, but the high degree of networking inside a company gives an intruder easy access to computers and important data in the company's local network.

The rising importance of networking is counterbalanced by the fact that even most system administrators can't keep pace with the rapid development of protocols and programs in the world of networks. Certainly we have all heard the buzzwords—RPC, Java, shttp, etc.—but who has time to delve into the technical details and to become familiar with all the daemons and services that are used, along with their faults? What is more, most of us lack formal education in the field of information security, so that many systems accessed via the Internet work with only rudimentary security mechanisms.

Across the board, this has made security a taboo subject, upholding the motto: "If we don't talk about how insecure we are, maybe no one will notice." This highlights a particular difficulty regarding security problems: any detailed information about a security hole is important for the system administrator, but in the wrong hands, that very information can stimulate curiosity simply to try out the described problem, just once. For this reason, security reports sometimes read like political speeches: we have a verbose overview of the problem, but the details are often missing. This creates an unsatisfactory situation for the system administrator who wants to understand *why* something poses a security problem.

SATAN: The Demise of the Internet?

At the end of 1993, the paper "Improving the Security of Your Site by Breaking into It" by Wietse Venema and Dan Farmer, authors of SATAN (Security Administrator's Tool for Analyzing Networks), created quite some excitement because it openly discussed security problems and gave clear instructions on how exploitation of system-related vulnerabilities permitted access to host computers. For the first time outside the hacker community, this paper provided a detailed report of how insecure some often-used services on the network really are and how easy it is to break into a UNIX system. When SATAN's release on April 5, 1995 provided a tool for automatic detection of such vulnerabilities, the news hit the media like a bomb.

"It's like randomly mailing automatic rifles to 5,000 addresses. I hope some crazy teen doesn't get a hold of one," wrote the *Oakland Tribune*. Other newspapers predicted the demise of the Internet, presumably in part because of the name SATAN.

As the number of intrusions did not rise measurably in the days after the release of SATAN and the feared catastrophes did not occur, the wave of panic subsided somewhat. Nevertheless, even today SATAN is still entwined in something of a myth that is difficult for experts to understand.

SATAN is a program that scans host computers for vulnerabilities caused by erroneous configurations or by known software errors in frequently used programs. SATAN detects these vulnerabilities and outputs a warning message along with an explanation of *why* each detected vulnerability represents a problem. SATAN does not intrude into computers; it is not a tool that allows an inexperienced cracker to gain access to a system with a mouse click. SATAN is an excellent tool for simply and comfortably conducting a security audit on a computer; however, the real power of SATAN emerges only when it is used for auditing a complete network with all connected computers and for depicting trust relationships between these computers along with their vulnerabilities.

Naturally SATAN can be abused. Any program and any publication that discusses security flaws can be abused. Nevertheless, the security problems that SATAN finds are nothing new; they were all known before the release of SATAN via publications, announcements of the Computer Emergency Response Teams (who provide assistance via the Internet when attempted intrusions occur), or mailing lists dedicated to system and network security. Indeed SATAN does not reveal vulnerabilities against which an administrator is helpless. On the contrary, SATAN provides information on how the detected vulnerabilities can be corrected.

This was the actual goal in the release of SATAN—to provide a tool that conducts security audits and to offer tips for correcting frequent vulnerabilities.

About This Book

This book describes how to install SATAN, how to configure it effectively, how to conduct security audits with it, and how to solve the detected problems. This is especially useful for system administrators of UNIX machines and for network administrators, but interested UNIX users on networks can also learn about secure configuration of their workstations.

Using SATAN requires a UNIX workstation with the graphical user interface X Windows and a browser for the World Wide Web (e.g., Internet Explorer, Mosaic, or Netscape). Root permissions on the workstation are also required; an unauthorized user can neither conduct the security audits nor correct the detected security flaws. Basic knowledge of UNIX system administration is necessary in order to utilize SATAN sensibly; extending and adapting SATAN to local requirements demands at least a basic knowledge of shell and Perl programming.

There is no patent remedy for network security. Although instructions can be given for correcting vulnerabilities, the actual brainwork always falls on the responsible network or system administrator, who must assess the danger in the local network and decide whether the potential danger justifies the cost of correcting it. Every network is different, and an acute danger in one network might prove to be something that another network administrator can live with.

This book goes beyond simply using SATAN off the shelf. SATAN can find only vulnerabilities that it has been programmed to detect. SATAN's modular structure enables extending its "knowledge" of vulnerabilities and adapting the program to local requirements. Furthermore, you can certainly defend against the abuse of SATAN, detect when a potential intruder employs this program against your host or network, and take appropriate measures.

Naturally, SATAN cannot detect every security vulnerability. In particular, there are security problems in the transfer protocols of the Internet and intranets, TCP/IP and UDP/IP, and in general in protocols based on IP. True security can be achieved only if all dangers are known, including those that SATAN cannot detect for purely technical reasons. Last but not least, security also depends on organization: without a security policy and planned measures in the event of a crisis, technical measures are of little help. To help you attain and maintain an integrated, secure operating concept and be ready with damage control if worse comes to worse, this book presents concise, practically oriented instructions for how to handle security in a network.

Organization

This book contains seven chapters and one appendix:

Chapter 1, *Security*, looks at some security basics: what network security is about, the technical side of security audits, what security tools are available.

Chapter 2, *Installing SATAN*, covers the system requirements for using SATAN, how to obtain, install, and compile SATAN, and special aspects of installing SATAN under Linux.

Chapter 3, *Security Audits*, describes configuring SATAN for a security audit, performing the audit, and evaluating the audit results.

Chapter 4, *Scan Results and Countermeasures*, discusses the security holes that SATAN tests, offers protective measures that can be taken if a weakness is detected, and looks at how critical the individual weaknesses are.

Chapter 5, *Extending and Adapting SATAN*, provides an inside view of how SATAN functions, suggests ways in which SATAN's capabilities can be extended, and describes how you can automate large scans.

Chapter 6, *Detecting and Repelling SATAN Attacks*, describes how to recognize when SATAN is being used by an intruder to detect flaws in your security, and how systems and networks can be protected against unauthorized access in general.

Chapter 7, *Beyond SATAN*, addresses vulnerabilities that SATAN cannot detect, and summarizes suggested steps in creating and implementing a security policy.

Appendix A, *Further Reading*, lists additional sources of information on computer security.

Conventions

Italic

> is used for file and directory names when they appear in the body of a paragraph and to emphasize new terms and concepts when they are introduced.

`Constant Width`

> is used in examples.

We'd Like to Hear from You

We have tested and verified all of the information in this book to the best of our ability, but you may find that features have changed (or even that we have made mistakes!). Please let O'Reilly know about any errors you find or suggestions for future editions by writing to:

> O'Reilly & Associates, Inc.
> 101 Morris Street
> Sebastopol, CA 95472
> 800-998-9938 (in U.S. or Canada)
> 707-829-0515 (international/local)
> 707-829-0104 (fax)

You can also send us messages electronically. To be put on the mailing list or request a catalog, send email to:

> *nuts@oreilly.com*

To ask technical questions or comment on the book, send email to:

> *bookquestions@oreilly.com*

Errata to Be and Examples

Though much effort has gone into making this book free of bugs, I suspect that some errors may have crept in nonetheless. You will be able to find an errata list and the example Perl script used in Chapter 4 on *ftp.rmi.de* in the directory */files/Satan-Book.* To retrieve them, use your favorite FTP client to log into *ftp.rmi.de* as user *anonymous* (do use *anonymous*: the commonly used login *ftp* will not work here) and use your email address as your password.

Acknowledgments

I owe gratitude to Walter Dörr, Frank Hoffmann, and Martina and Sven Kaschub for their support, their ideas, and our many discussions on security that went beyond the technical dimension. Special thanks go to Katrin Beckert and Hermann Heimhardt, without whose help (not to mention their notebook and workstation) this book would never have been done on time. I am also indebted to Elke Hansel and Gigi Estabrook of O'Reilly for their cooperation, to Bob Bach for doing most of the English translation, and of course to Dan Farmer and Wietse Venema for their review comments and for writing SATAN in the first place. Also at O'Reilly, I'd like to thank Clairemarie Fisher O'Leary for overseeing the production process, Nancy Wolfe Kotary for assisting with production, Ellie Maden and Sheryl Avruch for providing quality assurance, Robert Romano for creating all the figures, and Seth Maislin for creating the index.

1

Security

Before plunging into building and running SATAN, let's take a look at the basics: What is network security all about? How does a security audit work from the technical side? What other security tools are available?

What Is Security, Anyway?

As a systems or network administrator, or as a concerned user who has a login on a system running UNIX or another multiuser operating system, you have probably already asked yourself: Is my system secure? When I log in, are my files and my applications in the state in which I left them when I last used the system, or has someone modified them? Am I, in fact, the only person using that particular login or is somebody using my resources, pretending to be me?

Most people have this uneasy feeling at some time or other—I have, usually when looking at a file in my editor and muttering, "I could have sworn I made these changes yesterday—who's been meddling with my data?"

It is usually just forgetfulness on the user's part, or a simple mistake. I guess we have all done that—changed or deleted a file, and then wondered what happened when trying to access that file again a few days later. Sometimes, however, it may indeed be that someone has maliciously manipulated a file, changed your data, or caused your system to do unexpected things.

Security, then, is when things are as they seem to be, when your perception of what is going on matches reality. When things are different, when programs perform different tasks than you think they do, or files contain different data than what you put in them, you are in an insecure state: you do not know what has happened—or is still happening.

This of course begs the question: How do I find out if my system has been broken into? How do I determine if I am secure? How do I plug security holes, if they exist, and how do I find out if I have them in the first place?

In this book, I will focus on the last two of these questions, using SATAN as a tool to perform a network security audit, and give some tips on how to achieve better security. You will find good answers to the first question (and lots more) in Gene Spafford and Simson Garfinkel's excellent book *Practical UNIX & Internet Security*, also published by O'Reilly & Associates.

Be warned, though, that security is an elusive target. It is easy to find out if a particular vulnerability exists on a system or on a network. Proving that something is completely secure is a different thing altogether: that would mean testing a computer or network against an exhaustive checklist of vulnerabilities, and then proving that the checklist contains every known security problem.

Obviously, this is impossible. We have no way of guaranteeing absolute security. We can, however, do the next best thing: we can secure a system against a great many known attacks.

Why Network Security?

When thinking of security, most people think first of passwords. Passwords limit access to system resources (such as a login), and are used in most common operating systems, such as UNIX, Windows NT, or VMS. Using easily guessed passwords (such as your username, your girlfriend's name, your license plate number), or even not using a password at all, is of course almost an invitation to crack your account.

When thinking about security, file access permissions also spring to mind. If other users have read or write access to your data, or if users can execute programs that let them perform tasks that only root (the superuser) is normally allowed to do, that is also a security problem.

But while good password security and correct file permissions are critical to the security of your systems, there is still a problem—what about your network?

From a network perspective, security is more than just passwords and file permissions. Some of the problems encountered in network security are:

Design flaws in software or underlying network protocols
> Some network daemons, like *rexd*, a remote execution service, can easily be exploited to give an attacker the ability to run programs under (almost) any user ID, bypassing all the usual security mechanisms in UNIX. This is an

example of a poorly designed application: no matter how good the implementation of that program is, it can never be made secure.*

Insecure implementation of network software

Like all other software, a network program such as a mail transfer agent expects input in a specific format. If the software's author does not allow for the possibility that input to the program may not be in the expected format, strange things may happen. For example, overly long input may overflow a buffer, overwriting other variables in the program or causing the stack to be overwritten. If an attacker knows enough of the details of the application's implementation, he can alter its behavior, causing it to execute program code that he supplied, for example, in the body of an email message. Since many popular network services run under privileged user IDs, this may easily compromise your system.

Problems such as this are common: the design of the program might be good, but the actual coding is flawed.

Misconfiguration of network services

Correct configuration of some services is not easy, and the manual pages supplied by the vendor of the operating system are not always helpful—in fact, they sometimes supply inaccurate information. As a user or system administrator setting up an application, your goal is to get it to run, and you may not notice that the "standard" way of setting up an application allows an attacker to misuse it.

In network security, we have to move beyond the "security means good passwords" mindset. Most successful attacks against network services do not make use of passwords at all. While it is often the goal of an attacker to get the password file of a system she is trying to "crack," and thus to have an easier way of coming back later, it is possible to break into a computer without knowing a single password.

That said, of course passwords are important. It makes no sense to maximize network security and not care about system security at all. A sufficiently safe—from a system security point of view—computer is an essential building block when creating a secure network.

A Network Security Audit

How, then, does a network security audit work?

---

* Note that *rexd* security can be improved somewhat by using a more secure RPC (Remote Procedure Call) protocol. Not all operating systems support this, however.

Every program that performs security checks over a network needs to perform certain tasks, and SATAN is no exception. Broadly, during an audit, you need to find out:

- What computers are on the network
- What network services they offer
- If any of these services is insecure

What Computers Are on the Network?

The easiest way to find out if computers are reachable on a network is just to *ping* them, i.e., issue an ICMP Echo Request message (ICMP, the Internet Control Message Protocol, is part of the IP protocol suite) and see if you get a responding Echo Reply back. Thus, pinging all addresses of a known network results in a list of IP addresses that are "alive" and that warrant further inspection. SATAN uses the *fping* utility to do that; this program takes a list of IP addresses as command-line parameters and returns the list of addresses that respond.

One should bear in mind that *ping* is not a sure-fire way of finding every computer on a network—it is a way of finding every computer that is directly reachable, which is a different thing. A computer might not have an IP route back to you, or ICMP traffic (or even all IP traffic) might be blocked using filtering routers or other network devices. Scanning a network with pings will not return the addresses of those systems, and blindly relying on such a scan will mean that your security audit will miss those systems.

You can, of course, just run a full-featured check on every address in the network, whether it responds to pings or not. Indeed, SATAN can be configured to do just that. However, since checking a range of addresses that do not have a computer in them is just a sequence of waiting for time-outs, the time it takes to run SATAN will be prohibitive in large networks.

What Network Services Do They Offer?

Once you have a list of IP addresses that need to be checked, you will have to find out what network services are offered at these addresses. There is no magic way of finding out from a distance; to see if a service is running or not, the ports that are bound to these services need to be checked. Both TCP, the connection-oriented Transmission Control Protocol, and UDP, the connectionless User Datagram Protocol, employ port numbers to differentiate between different services running on the same computer. Think of ports like sockets for electrical power; if you have the right "plug," you can connect to the port and hence to the service running on it.

By scanning all the 65,536 ports available using both TCP and UDP, it is possible to get a complete picture of all the services running on a computer. If we send a packet to a port where no service is listening, we will receive either a request to terminate the connection (for TCP-based services) or the ICMP error message "port unreachable" (for UDP). If, on the other hand, there is an application listening on that port, there will be no error: the connection will succeed (for TCP) or the datagram (for UDP) will be silently accepted. Often we get a welcome banner or an error message from the application on that port—we get *something* back.

After this so-called port scan, we have a list of ports that are "open" and a list of the welcoming banners, error messages, or whatever was sent from each port. The port numbers themselves are not particularly helpful to the human performing the audit; what he needs is a list of services, e.g., FTP, WWW, gopher. Fortunately, the more frequently used services can be identified because they run on so-called well-known ports, as described in RFC 1700. On a UNIX system, you will also find a list of well-known ports in the file */etc/services*; on Windows 95, check \ *windows\services*. For example, port 21 is reserved for FTP, the File Transfer Protocol, just as port 80 is for WWW, port 25 for SMTP (electronic mail), and so on. Services that do not run on well-known ports can often be identified by the output they generate. A web server, for instance, can be identified by the fact that it sends text in HTML format. In this way, by parsing the output from each port, we can get information not only about what network applications are running, but also about the software that is used for these services. Most software has a characteristic footprint. For example, sendmail, by default, outputs a banner that details the version that is running, web servers often include their name and version numbers in error messages, and so on.

Are These Services Secure?

Some of the services detected can immediately be classified as insecure, like the *rexd* daemon mentioned earlier (we will go into more detail about *rexd* and other services in Chapter 4, *Scan Results and Countermeasures*). Other services need to be tested more thoroughly. For instance, if the port scan and subsequent analysis of the greeting banners show that sendmail in a particular version is running on a system, and that version is known to have security-related bugs or common misconfigurations, the security audit could start a subroutine that tries to exploit the bug. From the subroutine's output, we can deduce whether the bug is present.

But there is also a less technical side to security audits, which is: how are the audit results analyzed? While running a security scanner is easy, analyzing the output and determining how a reported vulnerability affects overall security is not. One other very real danger is that when you report to your manager that SATAN found no problems, she may conclude that you have a safe network. This is a daring assumption, and usually not true. Apart from the fact that any scanner can find only those security problems it knows about (that is, you might have problems that the scanner just could not detect), a "no problem" report can also mean that you picked the wrong tool for the job. Some firewall systems, for instance, are almost invisible to a security tool like SATAN.

What Else Is Out There?

While SATAN is the best-known tool for doing a security analysis of networks (and has certainly attracted the most media coverage), there are several other programs out there, both commercial and freeware, that do similar jobs. It is well worth taking a short look at them, if just to find out how they differ from SATAN:

- ISS v. 1.3 is a freely available program that performs a number of security checks on a range of IP addresses. After a port scan, it tries to exploit some well-known bugs in sendmail, find NFS (Network File System) partitions that are freely mountable, and check if *rsh* (remote shell) access is possible without a password. It also comes bundled with a program by Leendert van Doorn that tries to guess at NFS file handles. This version of ISS dates from 1994; it is the precursor of the commercial ISS program, which is much more powerful and which checks for a large number of both system-specific and general bugs in network software. ISS is available from *http://www.iss.net*; the freeware version is available from *ftp://ftp.iss.net/pub/iss*.

- Ballista is a relatively new commercial network security scanner from Secure Networks Incorporated (*http://www.secure.net*). I have no personal experience with this program.

- There is a plethora of port scanners around, both for UNIX and Windows systems, which are almost identical in the way they work. Some of the better ones (like jackal) use so-called half-open connections to scan TCP ports, which makes them more difficult to detect and also enables them to skip through some firewall systems.

In 1996, a program called phobia was floating around Usenet, author unknown. It is worth a mention not so much because of what it does regarding security checks (which is pretty much the same as ISS 1.3), as because of what else it does: it tries to open a TCP/IP connection to a certain IP address over the Internet and to send system information about the computer it is running on to that address.

This brings us to a very important point: *do not trust every program you find on the Internet.*

If you have the source, take a look at it before using the program. Try it on an isolated system first. When in doubt, or if you do not know or trust the source of a program, do not run it. Just as virus checkers are prime targets for writers of viruses, security scanners are ideal carriers for Trojan horses.

What Makes SATAN Different?

All of these programs perform in basically the same way: they do a port scan and perform a variety of tests on the services they find on each computer. What makes SATAN special—apart from its modular design, which makes it particularly easy to add new checks for security vulnerabilities—is that it does not treat each computer as a separate entity.

One very important concept in security is that of trust. Whenever computers are networked, a trust relationship is built between them. For example, when you work with your PC or your workstation, you will probably mount network drives from a server. There is a trust relationship here: you trust that the server is indeed *your* server, the one you usually use and not an impostor that has taken over the original server's identity and is now serving the wrong files to you.

But there are also less obvious examples of trust. When you log in to another system, you will normally not type the IP address of that system, but instead use a symbolic hostname or a fully qualified domain name, such as:

```
$ telnet ruby.ccnw.net
```

When doing this, you trust a DNS server to give you the correct IP address of *ruby.ccnw.net*. If the DNS server was taken over by an intruder, it might give you the wrong address, and you would end up logging into another system—and giving away your password to that system! You might not even notice that something is wrong when this happens if the intruder's system silently passes along everything you type to the system you originally wanted to connect to. This, by the way, is a so-called man-in-the-middle attack; an intruder is now silently listening in on your traffic.

Trust is everywhere. What SATAN attempts to do when scanning a network or multiple networks is to build a "web of trust," finding out what trust relationships exist between the computers on the network. This will show you what other targets an intruder might attack when security is compromised on one computer. You might be quite surprised to learn how many other computers your workstations extend trust to.

SATAN 2.0

As security is a moving target, SATAN will be updated to include checks for new security holes, and to offer a richer functionality. It is, of course, difficult to look into the future and predict exactly what will be in a future release, but these are the highlights.

What will be in the next version of SATAN?

- More checks in general, with a fair bit of testing WWW vulnerabilities. This should prove especially interesting; with new WWW servers being deployed at breathtaking speed everywhere, their security is often non-existent, as proven by the growing number of "hacked" servers. There will also be some testing of Windows NT–related security issues, which is a rapidly growing field of concern.

- The rulesets and conclusion engine will be spruced up.

- To enable faster scanning of networks, some of the checks that now run in sequence will be parallelized.

- There will be another level of problems. So far, SATAN is "binary" in its reports: you either have a security problem (red bullet) or you don't (black bullet). Some problems, however, are less pressing than others, so the next release of SATAN will have red, yellow, and black bullets.

- Where SATAN version 1 relied on the browser's capabilities for printing reports, i.e., you just printed out the HTML page, the next version will have support for printing both text and HTML reports.

2

Installing SATAN

I highly recommend that you compile SATAN yourself from the original sources, on the platform that you use for your security audits. While there are a lot of servers on the Internet that offer SATAN binaries, especially for Linux, you will never know for sure that what you get is actually a clean working version for your environment if you just grab a binary from somewhere. If you want to get to know SATAN in depth, perhaps even write your own modules for it, the additional time spent in compiling SATAN yourself is well worth it. You will get a much better understanding of how it works.

Where to Get SATAN

The newest version of SATAN is always available via anonymous FTP at *ftp.win.tue.nl* in the directory *pub/security.** This is a server of the Department of Mathematics and Computer Science at the Technical University of Eindhoven in the Netherlands, where Wietse Venema, co-author of SATAN, worked when SATAN was released (he is now at the IBM T. J. Watson Research Center).

Likewise, many CERTs (Computer Emergency Response Teams) have the latest version of the SATAN source code on their FTP or WWW servers. In Germany, for example, you will find SATAN on the FTP server of the CERT of the German Research Network (DFN), *ftp.cert.dfn.de*, in the directory */pub/tools/net*. In the United States, try *http://ciac.llnl.gov/ciac/ToolsUnixNetSec.html#Satan*; in Australia, have a look at *ftp://ftp.auscert.org.au/pub/coast/tools/unix/satan/satan*.

---

* As we go to press, the current version is SATAN 1.1.1.

To assure that you get an original version of SATAN, you really should obtain the source code from these FTP servers. Security tools are favorite targets of crackers[*] for Trojan horses[†] and similar cruelties. Particularly in regard to security audits, it is appropriate to be a little paranoid and to download the tools only from an official server. You should be especially warned against using precompiled binaries from unknown sources; although this saves you the trouble of compiling SATAN yourself, you run the risk of the program being a Trojan horse—you cannot see all that a binary file contains. Such a case for SATAN has already been documented: a Linux binary was infected. Therefore, I urge you to stay away from binary distributions.

If you use PGP,[‡] you have the additional option of verifying the authenticity of the SATAN sources with a digital signature. In addition to the tool SATAN, the server *ftp.win.tue.nl* in the directory */pub/security* contains the digital signature in the file *satan-1.1.1.tar.Z.asc*. Verify the authenticity of the sources simply by entering the following from the command line:

```
# pgp satan-1.1.1.tar.Z.asc
```

See the Appendix for Wietse Venema's PGP key fingerprint.

System Requirements

SATAN is not a standalone program, but a collection of various tools, some written in C, some in Perl, some in RPC. These tools probe for certain security flaws or search for hosts on the network. Additional Perl scripts analyze the output, structure it in small databases, and format it for screen output. SATAN creates HTML output; thus you need a web browser to view the results and to enter data via HTML forms.

Although you can read the web pages created by SATAN on an alphanumeric terminal (e.g., with *lynx*), an X terminal or a graphic console is highly recommended because it makes the output much more comprehensible. Likewise, a color monitor is recommended because it makes the distinction of the detected security flaws clearer; however, a monochrome monitor suffices.

To run SATAN you need the following:

---

[*] Originally the word "hacker" designated a respected computer expert who possessed in-depth knowledge in his/her area. "Cracker" or "dark side hacker" were terms for people who broke into others' programs or computers to abuse them for their purposes. Recently, common usage has merged the meanings of these two terms.

[†] A Trojan horse is a modification that makes a program do something other than what the user anticipates (deleting data, etc.).

[‡] PGP (Pretty Good Privacy) is an encoding and authentication program for files and email.

- A UNIX system with network access. SATAN has not been ported to other operating systems.

- A web browser on the host that is to run SATAN. For security reasons, you cannot use a browser running on a remote host (e.g., on a PC). The browser must support forms. Mosaic, Netscape, Chimera, Arena, and Lynx are examples of browsers that work with SATAN.

- Root (superuser) permissions on the UNIX system. Although data evaluation is possible under any user ID, execution of several SATAN scan programs requires access to system resources under the user ID *root.*

- Perl 5.000 or newer (*not* 5.000 alpha!). Perl is available for almost all UNIX variants; the newest version is available as source code at *http://www.perl.org.* Version 4 of Perl cannot be used with SATAN.

- A C development system.

- *rpcgen.* If this RPC compiler is not installed on the target system, you can use the *rpcgen* packaged with SATAN.

- X Windows.

In principle, SATAN can be run in batch mode via the command line, so that in dire straits you can get by without X Windows. However, in this mode only the basic security audits will function. Without a browser, you cannot view the classification and representation of results. In particular, without a Web browser you have no access to the SATAN documentation, so that you are not informed *why* a detected security flaw can be a problem.

For these reasons this book treats only SATAN's interactive mode. However, we can safely assume that today all modern UNIX systems have the X Windows system, so this certainly poses no problem.

Compiling and Installing SATAN

SATAN is distributed as a compressed *tar* file. Decompress and unpack it with the following command:

```
# uncompress < satan-1.1.1.tar.Z | tar xvf -
```

When you are done, the directory *satan-1.1.1* will contain various subdirectories, the files *satan* and *reconfig,* a Makefile, and a README file containing instructions for installing and launching SATAN.

```
# cd satan-1.1.1
# ls -F
Changes    bin/      perl/      rules/     /src
Makefile*  config/   perllib/   satan
README     html/     reconfig*  satan.8
TODO       include/  repent*    satan.ps
```

Running reconfig

First start the program *reconfig* with the following command:

```
# ./reconfig
```

reconfig attempts to find various UNIX commands, Perl, and a WWW browser in the filesystem; assuming that they are found, *reconfig* adapts the paths to these programs in SATAN's Perl scripts. Be sure that you really execute SATAN's *reconfig*; other software packages, such as the X server Xfree with Linux, also include a *reconfig* command for reconfiguring system parameters. Change to the SATAN directory before invoking *reconfig*, as in the above example.

Sometimes *reconfig* does not find all the required commands. This can occur, for example, if Perl does not have the anticipated filename or is not stored in the usual directory. In such cases you can directly edit the script *reconfig* and assign the Perl path name to the PERL variable.

Similarly, if you use a web browser other than Netscape, Mosaic, or Lynx, *reconfig* will report problems and you must enter a line in the file *config/paths.pl* before it will work. After *reconfig* terminates, identify your browser in the file *config/ paths.pl* by entering a line such as this one:

```
$MOSAIC="/usr/bin/X11/chimera";
```

This line redefines the Mosaic browser as the Chimera browser, so that SATAN will be able to find and execute this browser program later. While the variable name used to define the WWW browser is called MOSAIC, this does not restrict us to using Mosaic as a browser.

Compiling Needed Tools

After you have run *reconfig*, you still need to compile several tools that SATAN requires. Depending on the system, this might require some preparatory work, because three of these programs require header files that are missing in some systems, e.g., Linux: *tcp_scan*, *udp_scan*, and *fping*. The tools *tcp_scan* and *udp_ scan* are scan programs that probe which services are offered on which port numbers in the TCP or UDP protocol on a given host. *fping* is a program that "pings" all hosts in a subnetwork to determine which IP addresses are currently active on the network. For compilation, *tcp_scan*, *udp_scan*, and *fping* require header files conforming to BSD 4.4 for the IP protocol. Unfortunately, these files are not identical on all computers.

With SunOS, Solaris, and all newer System V UNIX systems, e.g., SINIX 5.42, compilation normally proceeds without problems (see Table 2-1 for a list of supported operating systems). On some other systems, you must manually adapt these header files. For Linux, you will find finished header files at *http://recycle.cebaf.gov/~doolitt/satan*. There you will also find additional information about using SATAN in the various Linux distributions. The header files must be unpacked in the directory *~satan/include/netinet*. (Check "Running SATAN Under Linux" later in this chapter for more information about running SATAN under Linux.)

Next, enter `make systemtype`. For SunOS 4.1.4, enter:

```
# make sunos4
```

On the basis of the specified system type argument, the program *make* then selects and executes the commands necessary for compiling SATAN for your system from the Makefile. The Makefile contains information about system libraries that SATAN needs, as well as definitions of system-specific variables and command-line options for the compiler.

This information is contained in the Makefile as rules with a corresponding line for every type of operating system.

Table 2-1 shows the Makefiles for the different operating systems.

Table 2-1. Supported Operating Systems

aix	IBM AIX
osf	DEC OSF
bsd	generic BSD 4.4
bsdi	BSDI
dgux	Data General UNIX
irix4	SGI IRIX 4
irix5	SGI IRIX 5
freebsd	FreeBSD
hpux9	HP-UX 9
linux	Linux; this might require some modifications; see the section "Running SATAN Under Linux" later in this chapter
sunos4	SunOS 4.1.x (Solaris 1)
sunos5	Solaris 2
sysv4	generic system V Release 4 (e.g., SINIX 5.42, Reliant Unix, ...)
ultrix4	Ultrix 4.x

For these operating systems, compilation can proceed without further work (with the possible exception of Linux, depending on the kernel version). If you use a different operating system, you first need to include a corresponding rule in the Makefile. Here it is easiest to adapt the rule for another operating system by complementing it with the necessary libraries, definitions, etc. Which specific modifications need to be made cannot be predicted on a general basis; this simply requires a bit of programming experience. For SCO UNIX, for example, modification takes the following form:

```
sco:
        @$(MAKE) all LIBS="-lsocket -lnsl" \
               XFLAGS="-DAUTH_GID_T=gid_t -DTIRPC"
```

Thereupon you can compile SATAN simply with *make sco*.

We're almost finished! However, two things still need to be observed.

Disabling Your Proxy Server

If your network is protected by a firewall,* the WWW browser must be configured so that it uses *no* proxy services. When a firewall is used, WWW browsers are normally configured so that their connection to the Internet is indirect, occurring via a proxy server. A proxy is a special process on the firewall that retrieves the WWW page requested by the local browser from the Internet and forwards it to the requesting host. In this way the computers behind the firewall do not require their own direct Internet connection, which significantly increases security.

However, for security reasons SATAN does not allow the use of a proxy server. Data transfer between SATAN and the WWW browser must take place directly so that it cannot be intercepted. Therefore, you must disable the use of a proxy server in the browser configuration. The settings can be found in the menu Options → Network Preferences (for Netscape 3), Edit → Preferences → Advanced → Proxies (for Netscape Communicator) or in the browser's application defaults (directory */usr/lib/X11/app-defaults/...*). For Mosaic you need to delete the following lines in the file */usr/lib/X11/app-defaults/Mosaic*:

```
Mosaic*httpProxy:      http://www.dg5kx.de/
Mosaic*ftpProxy:       http://www.dg5kx.de/
Mosaic*waisProxy:      http://www.dg5kx.de/
Mosaic*gopherProxy:    http://www.dg5kx.de/
Mosaic*newsProxy:      http://www.dg5kx.de/
Mosaic*fileProxy:      http://www.dg5kx.de/
```

(The name of your proxy server will be different from that in the example.) Before you begin deletions, make a backup of the file. If Mosaic is running, you need to quit and restart it in order for modifications to take effect.

For a different browser, check its documentation in case of doubt.

---

* A firewall is a specialized host that protects against intrusions from the Internet or other networks.

Using DNS

If your workstation does not use DNS (Domain Name Service), set the following entry in the file *~satan/config/satan.cf* from 0 to 1:

```
$dont_use_nslookup = 0;
```

Afterwards it should read as follows:

```
$dont_use_nslookup = 1;
```

You can recognize that a system uses DNS by the presence of the file */etc/resolv.conf.* If this file contains an entry for a name server, then in principle DNS can be used. Test whether DNS is actually running with the command *nslookup.* It makes sense to use DNS because this makes SATAN's output much easier to read due to the use of the complete host and domain name instead of only the IP address.

Although you can still toggle the use of DNS on and off later via SATAN's configuration menu, if this entry is incorrect SATAN cannot even start up. SATAN employs its own Web server to output its results and permits connections to this server only from the workstation where SATAN was launched. If DNS is not functioning, even though it may be enabled in *satan.cf,* SATAN cannot determine the IP address of its own workstation, and the Web server fails to launch.

Starting SATAN

Now our configuration is complete. Invoking *./satan* from X Windows launches SATAN. SATAN independently starts the specified WWW browser and all other tools it needs. Netscape, Mosaic, etc. need not be started in advance.

If you use Netscape Version 3 or newer as your browser, then before starting SATAN you need to make a small modfication. This modification is described in the subsection "Using Netscape with SATAN," later in this chapter.

Repent!

If the name SATAN bothers you, you can change it to something less diabolical. Running the *repent* program supplied with SATAN will change all occurrences of SATAN in the program and the documentation to SANTA (Security Analysis Network Tool for Administrators), which sounds much nicer. You will have to run *repent* before issuing the *make* command.

In this book, however, we will continue to refer to the program as SATAN, as that is what everybody knows it as.

(And yes, the picture of Satan is changed to Santa's picture, too.)

Running SATAN Under Linux

Beyond lacking BSD 4.4-conforming header files,* Linux can pose certain other difficulties. This is not the fault of SATAN, but of Linux; the internals of Linux deviate somewhat from other UNIX operating systems. Due to the multitude of different distributions and kernel variants, it is impossible to provide a generally applicable recipe, but we do address some of the common problems here.

For example, the script *reconfig* might fail to start and the shell might report an error on execution. This is because *bash*, the default shell under Linux, cannot handle the mechanism that *reconfig* uses to determine whether it is being executed under Perl or under the shell. This is easy to solve: start *reconfig* under Perl rather than directly from the shell:

```
# perl ./reconfig
```

Alternatively, you can place the comment character # in front of the first line of *reconfig*.

Beware of the program of the same name that is part of Xfree! On installation, start *reconfig* with *./reconfig* (if you are in the correct directory) or with the absolute path name; otherwise you might start the wrong *reconfig* program by mistake.

The system function *select()* is implemented somewhat differently in Linux than in other UNIX systems, which can cause problems with the tool *tcp_scan*. You will find a patch to solve this problem at the URL *http://recycle.cebaf.gov/~doolitt/satan/tcp_scan.diff2*.

We recommend not using SATAN under Linux with an underconfigured PC: a 486 with 16 MB memory is the minimum. On slow machines you might run into timing problems, especially with the tool *fping*. This is the case if SATAN terminates its scan of a subnetwork with the following message even though the networked computer is active:

```
...get_targets failed -- unable to expand subnet ...
```

You can circumvent this by not scanning complete networks, but individual hosts instead. Naturally, this uncomfortably restricts SATAN's functionality, so it is better to increase the timeout values. In the file *~satan/perl/targets.pl*, in the function *target_acquisition*, raise the timeout:

```
sub target_acquisition
{
local($target, $proximity, $level) = @_;
local($targets_found);
```

---

* These header files can be downloaded from *http://recycle.cebaf.gov/~doolitt/satan*.

```
# Expand and then collect. Pass results through new_target() for
# consistent handling of constraints and policies.
&open_cmd (TARGETS, 120, "$GET_TARGETS $target");
while (<TARGETS>) {
...
```

In the command *open_cmd*, the default value for the second parameter is 120 seconds as a static value. It is a good idea to replace this value with the variable *$long_timeout*. The value of this variable can then be modified either interactively via the Web browser in SATAN's configuration menu or alternatively in SATAN's configuration file (described in the section "SATAN's Configuration File (satan.cf)" in Chapter 5, *Extending and Adapting SATAN*).

Network newsgroups have reported other problems, such as parsing the output of *showmount* (a tool that displays which filesystems an NFS server exports) and buffer overflows in the Linux network software. Newer Linux distributions (kernel version 2) apparently do not produce these errors.

Things That Might Go Wrong

This section identifies problems you might encounter when using SATAN.

Using Netscape with SATAN

Many people have reported problems using SATAN together with the Netscape WWW browser. The usual symptom is that SATAN starts up all right, but clicking on one of the hyperlinks in the control panel does not show the page that is expected, but instead pops up a window asking where to save that page.

This happens because most of the pages that SATAN displays in the Web browser are not static HTML documents. Instead, SATAN uses Perl scripts that generate the HTML output you see on the fly. In its default installation, Netscape 3 recognizes these scripts by their extension "pl" and attempts to save the document rather than running the script and displaying its output.

To change this behavior, click on the menu item Options → General Preferences and then the panel *Helpers*. In the table located there, the left column describes a file type (where the format of the descriptions corresponds to a MIME content type, a standard for describing document contents that is also used for electronic mail). Find the entry *application/x-perl,* select it with a mouse click, and click the Edit button on the right. In the dialog window that appears, simply delete the suffix entry "pl" for Perl and click the OK button. This deactivates the Perl entry, and Netscape can be used with SATAN. In later versions of the Netscape browser, this dialog has been moved to Edit → Preferences → Navigator → Applications.

Can't Find All My Network Addresses

When your screen looks like this when starting SATAN:

```
# ./satan
SATAN is starting up....
Unable to find all my network addresses
#
```

something is wrong with your DNS configuration (if, indeed, you are using DNS at all), with your NIS configuration, or with your */etc/hosts* file.

For security reasons, SATAN will talk only to a WWW browser that is running on the local host. To find out if the browser is indeed local, one of SATAN's Perl scripts determines all the IP addresses your workstation has. When a connection is established to SATAN's own WWW server from a browser that is not from one of these IP addresses, SATAN deduces that someone else is trying to grab the information from a SATAN run, and terminates after giving out a warning message.

Make sure that DNS or NIS is configured properly. If all else fails, configure SATAN not to use DNS by setting the **dont_use_nslookup** entry in the file *~satan/config/satan.cf* to 1:

```
$dont_use_nslookup = 1;
```

Make sure that there is an entry in your */etc/hosts* file containing your own IP address(es) and your own hostname.

Can't Find My Own Hostname

If, upon startup, SATAN dies with the message

```
# ./satan
SATAN is starting up....
Can't find my own hostname: set $dont_use_nslookup in config/satan.cf
#
```

then SATAN was unable to determine the name of your workstation. Disabling the use of DNS (as in the problem described above) will cure this if your own hostname appears in */etc/hosts*.

SATAN tries to find the name of your host by using the *hostname*, *uname*, and *uuname* commands. If these commands are in a strange directory on your workstation, take a look at *~/perl/hostname.pl* and try changing the paths to these commands.

3

Security Audits

We will take a look at how to configure SATAN here, and I'll present a sample audit performed on a heterogenous network. It is important to get the configuration right: just installing SATAN and giving it a quick try, without prior careful thought about its configuration, is a dangerous thing. Besides the fact that you might get misleading or even outright false information out of an audit if you have not configured SATAN correctly—after all, the old garbage in, garbage out adage applies to SATAN too—SATAN is a dangerous tool just to let loose on a network. You might start scanning systems that do not even belong to you, which will not make you a very popular person in your company or on the Internet.

The Control Panel

Start SATAN by simply entering the following command in X Windows:

```
# ./satan
```

A few seconds after you launch SATAN, you will see the control panel (see Figure 3-1).

If you do not see this panel, or if you get error messages either from SATAN or from your WWW browser (or if you do not see anything at all), check the section "Things That Might Go Wrong" in Chapter 2, *Installing SATAN*.

The control panel allows you to set the following:

* How SATAN manages the data it collects

* Which targets to scan

* How to analyze collected data and how to generate reports

* How to configure SATAN

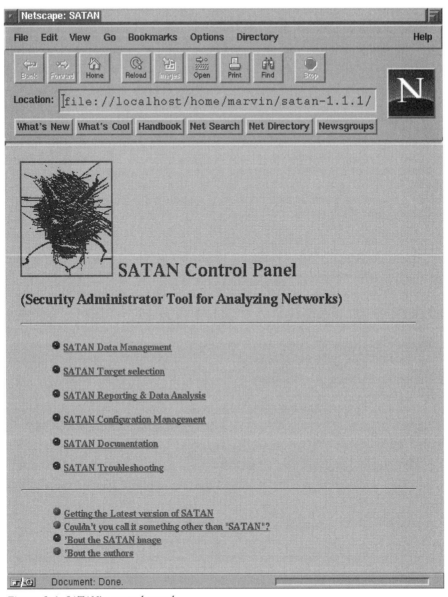

Figure 3-1. SATAN's control panel

In addition, the control panel contains hyperlinks to the documentation, which is well worth reading, and to the tutorials on network and system security. You will also find tips on getting SATAN running in case you have difficulties, and information on obtaining the latest version of SATAN, about the authors, etc.

Data Management

First select the link "SATAN Data Management." (If you use Netscape version 3 or newer and find yourself confronted with a dialog window instead of an HTML form, read the section "Using Netscape with SATAN" in Chapter 2 for information on how to configure Netscape 3 so that it can handle the HTML pages that SATAN generates.) In the Data Management HTML form, you can select the database in which to store SATAN's results in the subsequent security audits or from which to read the results of previous security audits. A "database" for SATAN is a collection of plain text files residing in the directory *~satan/results/<database name>*.

If you are scanning only one or two computers, you can leave the default name, *satan-data*. However, for a security audit on a larger network, such as a company or campus network, it makes sense to create a separate database for each subnetwork. Otherwise, when auditing hundreds of hosts, it is difficult to preserve an overview of which machines on which networks are particularly vulnerable. The databases can easily be merged afterwards (in the "Merge existing SATAN databases" option) for a combined view of the overall network.

In the first text field, enter the name of the new database to be created. To open an existing database, simply click on its name; all existing databases are displayed under the text field as hyperlinks. Proceed similarly to append the data of one database to an existing database: in the text field "Merge with existing SATAN database" enter the name of the database or select it from the list of existing hyperlinks under the text field.

After you press the Enter key or click on the corresponding button, SATAN reads the database; this can take a while if the database contains numerous hosts. SATAN displays a message after completing the read operation. Click on "Back to the SATAN start page" to return to the main menu.

The next link in the control panel is "SATAN Target selection" (with subsequent start of the scan), but before you proceed, you need to configure SATAN so that your scan will work properly.

Configuring SATAN

Unfortunately, "SATAN Configuration Management" is the fourth menu item in the main menu. This induces you to go directly to "Target Selection" and to start up the security audit immediately after you select the database in the first menu item. Don't do it!

SATAN's default settings are not the most aggressive, but even so, they can draw the attention of an alert system administrator. Especially if you are working with a version of SATAN that you did not install yourself, you need to check the configuration settings. SATAN can potentially check not only your selected targets, but also hosts that share some trust relationship with these targets: DNS servers, YP servers, or any host that offers services on which your original target relies. Perhaps without even noticing it right away, you could easily set SATAN loose on hosts of your Internet service provider or your computing center. This may mean that you have to face uncomfortable questions, if not legal consequences.

However, even without considering external hosts, you first need to adapt some SATAN settings to local requirements, or your results will not be particularly meaningful. For example, SATAN needs to know what relationship the host on which it is running has to other hosts on the network—whether it appears in *.rhosts* files, whether filesystems are imported via NFS, etc. If these specifications are not made before a scan, SATAN might report vulnerabilities that do not actually exist.

Storing the Collected Data

Configuration Management first asks where the collected data is to be stored. This directory is the same as the database selected under Data Management, so normally the directory suggested here is appropriate.

Selecting a Probe Level

Next, select SATAN's probe level ("What probe level should I use?"): light, normal, or heavy.

A light scan probes the DNS entries for the selected targets and determines which RPC services the target offers and which filesystems it exports via NFS. Normally this scan is not noticed on the target system unless special security mechanisms are implemented there. For example, a wrapper (protective software) might log incoming requests to *rpcbind*. Such a wrapper, like the *tcp wrapper* that we discuss later, can protect a system quite effectively against attacks, and thus also against SATAN, and can detect whether a SATAN scan is currently in progress.

The normal scan additionally tests the availability of common network services such as gopher, WWW, finger, Telnet or rlogin, FTP, and email. From the greeting banners of the various services that it finds, SATAN can also determine the type and version of the operating system. This is important information, since certain operating system versions have well-known vulnerabilities that an attacker could exploit. However, this probe level may leave traces in the log files of the individual services.

Normally you would employ a heavy scan for a security audit in your own network; only this level finds all the vulnerabilities that SATAN is capable of detecting. Remember to inform the administrators of the systems to be audited so that they do not worry needlessly when irregularities occur.

A heavy scan enhances the attained knowledge of the provided services. For example, if SATAN detects that a target is running FTP, SATAN tests whether anonymous FTP is enabled and whether the anonymous FTP home directory is writable (a common configuration error). If the target provides an X Windows server, SATAN tests whether the access control mechanisms for X.11 have been activated. At this probe level SATAN finds the most vulnerabilities. However, a heavy scan is easy for the system administrator of the target system to detect. The scan not only leaves messages in the log files of the individual processes, it also normally triggers warning messages on the console (thus alerting not only system administrators, but also end users on workstations). A heavy scan also probes many TCP and UDP ports on the targets for proprietary servers. Due to the unusually high number of attempted connections, routers might trigger alarms in the network management. Many network components provide for the setting of threshold values; when these are exceeded, the management system is notified via the SNMP protocol.

Which scans are executed at which probe level is specified in detail in SATAN's central configuration file, *~satan/config/satan.cf.* Chapter 4, *Scan Results and Countermeasures*, discusses how to adapt SATAN to local requirements and how to change the default settings.

Setting Timeouts and Terminating Processes

The timeout values, the next field in the configuration form, can normally be left at the default values. These values serve to accelerate SATAN. On a scan for services, if SATAN fails to find a service, for example, because a filtering router or a filtering bridge on the network fails to forward the respective protocol, there would normally be a long wait for the corresponding subprocess itself to reach a timeout. After the specified time value expires, SATAN itself terminates such a process by sending it a KILL signal.

By default the middle timeout value is set for all subprocesses. However, several processes, especially the RPC services, prove significantly slower in their reaction time and thus require the higher values provided by the *slow timeout* setting.

Timeout values should be increased if you work with slow or very overloaded network paths, such as an analog dial-in modem connection, or slow dedicated lines on the Internet or in your internal network. For LAN connections the default values are quite reasonable and need not be changed.

Which signal SATAN uses to terminate processes is set in the next field. The KILL signal under UNIX is normally 9.

Recognizing Trust Relationships

The next field concerns one of the most interesting features of SATAN, its recognition of trust relationships between hosts. SATAN can not only audit individual hosts or complete subnetworks, but also recognizes which other hosts have some trust relationship to the target systems. These could be DNS servers, clients that import a filesystem, hosts that appear on execution of the *finger* command, etc. These hosts can also be tested automatically with SATAN. This has two consequences. First, you can find vulnerabilities on these hosts that affect the primary targets of the security audit; for example, if the DNS server of a host is vulnerable, this opens unsuspected opportunities for also disabling the clients that use this server. Second, these secondary targets have relationships (i.e., trust) with other hosts, which can then be audited as well.

In this way SATAN can record a logical network of dependencies that often leads to surprising results. Relationships between hosts in large networks are traditionally poorly documented and difficult to record and maintain because they are so dynamic. Especially in NFS networks that employ *automount*, it is nearly impossible to predict which hosts will be communicating with which others at any given time or which hosts are affected when a server crashes for whatever reason. Aside from the security aspects of such trust relationships, SATAN affords an excellent means of creating a sort of logical map that represents the network structure at application level, independent of the physical structure of the network.

Deciding How Far to Probe

The field "How far out from the original target should I probe?" puts a ceiling on the extent to which you want to continue this snowball effect. Here the *maximal proximity* is the greatest *logical* distance.

If you enter 0, as in Figure 3-2, only the direct target hosts or subnetworks are scanned. A value greater than 0 specifies the permitted depth of dependency nesting; 1 allows hosts dependent on the original target to become new targets; 2 continues the scan on hosts dependent on these new targets.

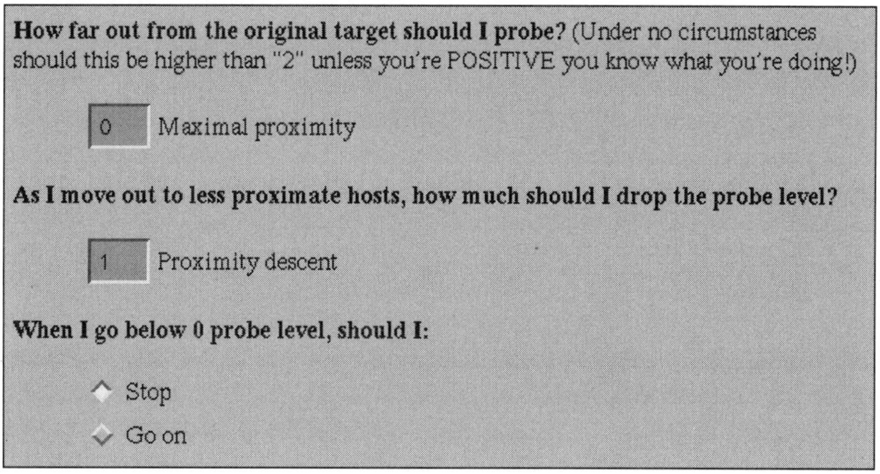

How far out from the original target should I probe? (Under no circumstances should this be higher than "2" unless you're POSITIVE you know what you're doing!)

    0   Maximal proximity

As I move out to less proximate hosts, how much should I drop the probe level?

    1   Proximity descent

When I go below 0 probe level, should I:

    ◇ Stop

    ◇ Go on

Figure 3-2. Configuring the audit of independent computers

WARNING   Here we have a potential bomb: it is easy to recognize that the number of hosts to be scanned rises exponentially with a rising proximity value. With a proximity of 1 you can still predict relatively well what will happen and which hosts will be affected; frequently, a value of 2 already brings in hostnames that were unforeseen. Higher values produce uncontrolled expansion of the scan. You should never select a value larger than 2 if there is an Internet connection; otherwise you might be trying to tackle the entire Internet.

For a security audit on a network that is protected by a firewall or completely decoupled from the Internet, a proximity value greater than 2 can return interesting results. To get acquainted with SATAN, however, you should begin with 0 and then increase the proximity value incrementally. Starting small also reduces the deluge of data to be evaluated afterwards.

The *proximity descent* specifies the value for decrementing the probe level for dependent hosts (indirect targets). It makes sense to lightly scan hosts that are farther away; after all, the scan results of the primary targets are more interesting. Here 1 is a sensible value; 0 would mean that indirect targets would be scanned with the same probe level as primary targets.

If the probe level drops below 0 (becomes less than a light scan), you can choose whether SATAN should terminate scans of the respective targets or whether the audit should continue as light scans.

Scanning a Subnetwork

Optionally, SATAN can run a security audit on a whole subnetwork rather than on a single host. Here SATAN uses *ping* to determine which hosts are connected to the network and then scans them. In the next field, this *subnet expansion* can be enabled. This especially makes sense if a firewall network that is to be audited might contain multiple hosts that lack DNS entries. This often occurs with the use of *split-horizon* DNS; i.e., DNS entries propagated within the network differ from those propagated onto the Internet. Just as an attacker would do, SATAN can determine whether hidden hosts are present. However, this also harbors the danger that targets are scanned that should not be scanned at all. If an Internet domain is the target of a security audit, note that enabling *subnet expansion* can easily lead to scanning hosts outside this domain. Although a domain name is frequently identical to its network address, this is not an absolute requirement.

WARNING   For SATAN, a subnetwork is not necessarily identical to the IP subnetwork that is used in the network. On a subnetwork expansion, the whole Class C network in which a host resides (or the corresponding subnetwork with the network mask 255.255.255.0 if a Class A or Class B address is being audited) becomes the target. SATAN knows nothing about subnetting or supernetting, and if your own network uses a network mask other than 255.255.255.0, you should be aware that SATAN's view of the network structure differs from the real one!

Is this a Trusted Host?

Now you need to set whether the host on which SATAN is running is a *trusted host*, that is, recorded in *.rhosts*, *hosts.equiv*, or similar files in a target system. If so, you do not need to check whether remote shell access is possible since access is explicitly enabled. Click on the corresponding button to indicate whether SATAN is running on a *trusted host*. It makes sense to conduct a security audit from an *untrusted host*, since a potential intruder would be doing the same.

Limiting the Scope of the Audit

You can generally restrict the scans to certain domains or subnetworks (see Figure 3-3) by entering the name, domain suffix, or network address of targets to be scanned in the field "Patterns specifying hosts to limit the probe to." Thereupon SATAN scans only targets in the specified domains or in the specified networks. In this way, you should restrict your first SATAN security audit to your own hosts.

Patterns specifying hosts to limit the probe to
If you only want to probe hosts within a specific domain, you could use, for example:
podunk.edu
If you only want to probe sites on a particular subnet, you could use, for example:
192.9.9
sni.de 192.109.2 siemens.de sbs.de

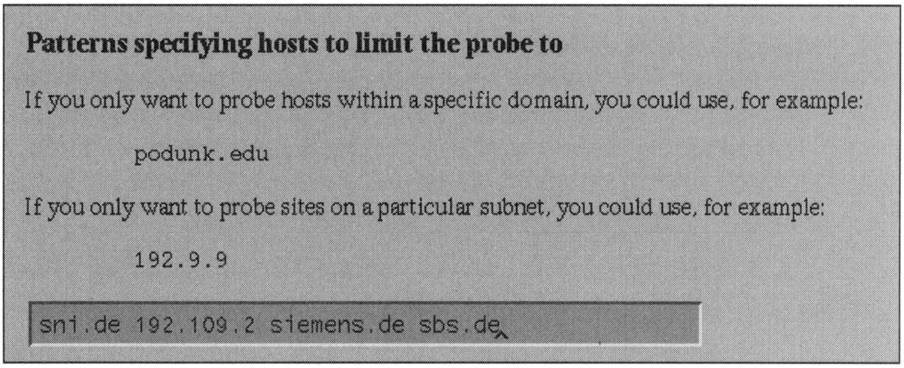

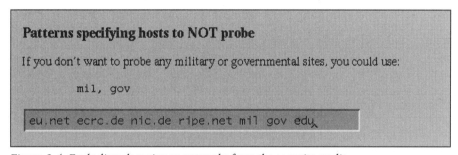

Figure 3-3. Limiting the scans to individual domains and subnetworks

You can formulate the restriction on targets to scan differently: in general, scan all hosts, but exclude certain domains or networks. Enter this formulation in the next field (see Figure 3-4).

Patterns specifying hosts to NOT probe
If you don't want to probe any military or governmental sites, you could use:
mil, gov
eu.net ecrc.de nic.de ripe.net mil gov edu

Figure 3-4. Excluding domains or networks from the security audit

Normally, it is a good idea to enter the hosts of your Internet service provider here so that the provider does not get alarmed during your security audit. Likewise the networks of customers, suppliers, research institutes, etc. should be entered here if you know that there is a communication relationship, but you do not want to sic SATAN on their networks. Otherwise the proximity mechanism described earlier can cause an unpleasant situation. A scan of network trust relationships often returns unexpected results. A pitfall of SATAN is that often you don't discover which hosts you have unintentionally scanned until you evaluate the scan data.

Using nslookup and ping

Last but not least, two additional settings influence SATAN's work. First, specify whether a functioning DNS server is available, i.e., whether SATAN may use the command *nslookup* to resolve names in IP addresses. If you do not employ DNS, click on the button "DNS is unavailable."

Next, you must decide whether SATAN may use *ping* to determine whether hosts on the network are active. *ping* employs the Internet Control Message Protocol (ICMP) and serves as a sort of echo function: a host on the network will always send a response to a *ping* packet. This is an excellent way to determine whether a host is accessible under an IP address, and saves SATAN a lot of work in scanning complete networks. First, *ping* can determine which addresses are occupied, i.e., which hosts are on the network at all, and then SATAN can concentrate its scans on these hosts. This is important because IP networks are often sparsely populated; i.e., few of their addresses are occupied. Testing all addresses in an IP network would cause many a timeout.

Unfortunately—or, from a security perspective, we should say fortunately—this does not work on every network. The ICMP protocol permits a number of activities (following routes with *traceroute*, changing routes using ICMP to redirect packets, etc), which is why this protocol is often blocked by filtering routers. If you know that this is the case in your network, click on the button "Don't ping hosts: ICMP does not work." SATAN then assumes that all addresses correspond to hosts and attempts to scan these hosts whether they exist or not.

Congratulations! SATAN should now be set up and you can begin. Click on the button "Change the configuration file" to save the changes you made. SATAN then confirms the successful update of the configuration file *satan.cf.* Click on "Back to the SATAN start page" to return to the control panel.

Selecting and Scanning a Target

Next, enter the target of your security audit, either the name of a host, an IP address, or a network address. In the latter case, SATAN tries to find and scan all hosts on the network. If you enter a hostname, then under the input field you can specify whether only the specified host or its entire subnetwork is to be scanned. Furthermore, you can once again set the probe level for scanning—light, normal, or heavy, as described in the section "Configuring SATAN," earlier in this chapter.

Click on the button "Start the scan." In the background SATAN launches the subprocesses that handle the actual work and displays their execution (depending on your browser, either at run time or at the end of the scan). Depending on the number of targets to be scanned and the speed of the network connection, this can take several minutes to several hours, so be patient. There is not much to see while a scan is in progress.

SATAN lets you know when the scan is complete. On the HTML page you can see when the individual subprocesses were started and with which options. Figure 3-5 shows the output after scanning a single target.

SATAN data collection

Data collection in progress...

```
14:32:28 bin/timeout 120 bin/get_targets marvin
14:33:08 bin/timeout 120 bin/tcpscan.satan 1-9999 marvin
14:33:29 bin/timeout 120 bin/udpscan.satan 1-2050,32767-33500 marvin
14:33:34 bin/timeout 20 bin/udpscan.satan 53,177 marvin
14:33:34 bin/timeout 20 bin/finger.satan marvin
14:33:41 bin/timeout 20 bin/tcpscan.satan 70,80,ftp,telnet,smtp,nntp,uucp,6000 marvin
14:33:53 bin/timeout 20 bin/dns.satan marvin
14:33:54 bin/timeout 20 bin/rpc.satan marvin
14:33:55 bin/timeout 20 bin/xhost.satan -d marvin:0 marvin
14:33:56 bin/timeout 20 bin/ftp.satan marvin
14:33:57 bin/timeout 20 bin/rusers.satan marvin
14:33:58 SATAN run completed
```

Data collection completed (1 host(s) visited).

Back to the SATAN start page I Continue with report and analysis I View primary target results

Figure 3-5. SATAN data collection

You can see that the host *marvin* was scanned. After the invocation of *bin/get_ targets*,[*] the portscanner for TCP/IP and UDP/IP was started to determine which services were active on the host. For efficiency reasons, by default not all 65,536 possible ports were probed, but only the interesting ones, i.e., the standard or usual ports where services run.

Next, individual services were examined more precisely: finger, DNS, RPC, X.11 (*xhost*), FTP, and *rusers*.

With "View primary target results" you can directly view the results of the scan, or with "Continue with report and analysis" you can jump to the report-generating page. Let us see what SATAN found out about *marvin* (see Figure 3-6) and save the general analysis for later.

---

[*] A Perl script that establishes the names and IP addresses of all targets to be scanned (in the example, an easy task with only a single host).

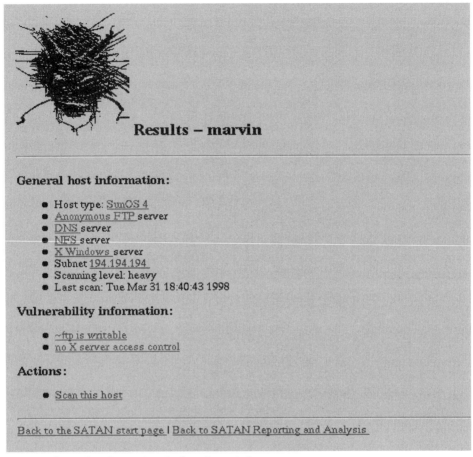

Figure 3-6. Results of scanning the host "marvin"

Under the heading "General host information," you will find data on the scanned system. SATAN has determined that the target is a Sun workstation running the operating system SunOS 4.x. This Sun is also running an anonymous FTP server, a DNS server, and X Windows. Additionally, we see to which subnetwork the host is connected, the probe level of the scan, and when the last scan took place. The last two items prove interesting if you want to regularly scan a larger number of hosts; this helps to retain an overview of how current the information in the database is.

Under "Vulnerability information," you see the weaknesses that SATAN detected. In our example these are an anonymous FTP with a writable home directory (a serious vulnerability) and an X server with no access control; i.e., any client can take over the monitor, the keyboard, and the mouse and see everything on the monitor. In Chapter 4, *Scan Results and Countermeasures*, we discuss these individual vulnerabilities, their meanings, and possible countermeasures.

Once you've corrected the erroneous configurations that caused the problems, you can check the effectiveness of your corrections by rescanning the host; click on the action "Scan this host."

Almost all of the data collected on a host is represented as hyperlinks. Simply clicking on an item in the "General host information" section takes you to the database, where you can display other hosts that use the same operating system or that are also DNS servers, etc. In this way the administrator can quickly gain an overview of which hosts on the network offer a certain service.

Click on "Back to SATAN Reporting and Analysis" (or the link "SATAN Reporting & Data Analysis" in the control panel) to go to the overview menu for data analysis.

Analyzing the Scan Results

One of SATAN's great advantages over other security tools is its ability to manage the security-related data that it finds and to sort them by any criteria. If you are administering only a few hosts, this capability might not be so important; you can probably remember when you audited the last two or three hosts and which vulnerabilities were detected. By contrast, a plagued network administrator managing 100 or even 1000 hosts and who wants to maintain an overview can appreciate SATAN's data management capabilities.

Company management sometimes lacks affection for regular security audits, because they take time and afford no immediately visible return on investment. Therefore, system and network administrators often squeeze audits in between other duties, whenever they find time. As a result, the documentation of the security status of systems on the network almost always suffers. SATAN's data analysis menu can fill that gap by affording a good means of achieving a quick overview of the status of a network.

You can display the contents of the current database in three ways. The contents can be sorted by:

- Vulnerabilities
- General host information
- Trust

Within each of these items, you can specify various sorting criteria.

After SATAN has completed a scan, you will first want to know which systems have vulnerabilities—indeed, this is why you ran SATAN. You should first list the systems sorted by the number of vulnerabilities found (vulnerability count). Here all scanned hosts are listed by name or, if the name was not found, by IP address. Hosts with detected vulnerabilities are marked with a red dot. For each host, the number in parentheses after the hostname tells you how many vulnerabilities were found.

You can configure the marks that SATAN uses to indicate vulnerabilities. This is especially helpful with a monochrome monitor, so that the marks are clearly distinguishable. In this book we substitute an exclamation mark for the red dot so that in our black-and-white figures you can distinguish it from the black dot that marks a secure host. The various icons that SATAN uses reside in the directory *~satan/html/dots*; for this book we replaced *reddot.gif* with a GIF image of an exclamation mark.

Let us examine the Data Analysis menu of an actual scan of a subnetwork with about 200 hosts (see Figure 3-7). Our hybrid subnetwork contains a colorful mix of UNIX and Windows NT servers, workstations under UNIX and various MS Windows versions, and various routers and other active network components. The hostnames and IP addresses have been changed (to protect the innocent), so don't get your hopes up. :-) The actual effects of these vulnerabilities and how to correct them are discussed in detail in Chapter 4.

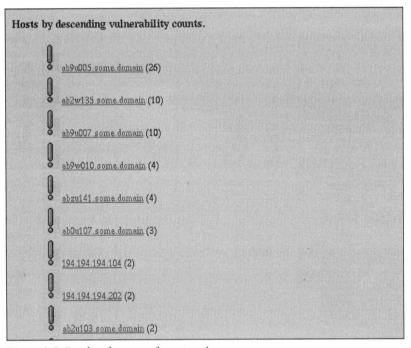

Figure 3-7. Results of a scan of a network

In Figure 3-7, the first three hosts are conspicuous due to their unusually high vulnerability counts. Such counts usually result when a host exports many filesystems via NFS without access restrictions, since SATAN counts each unrestricted export as a separate vulnerability.

By clicking on a hostname, you obtain more detailed information about this host, such as that shown in Figure 3-6 for the host *marvin*. Then by selecting one of the hyperlinks under "General host information" you can display all hosts on the scanned network that share the selected attribute. This is a fast means of displaying all DNS servers on the network, for example.

All detected vulnerabilities are also displayed as hyperlinks under the heading "Vulnerability information." By selecting one of these links, you display information about the respective vulnerability and tips for correcting it; this is useful for quickly determining why a displayed vulnerability is a problem. This information can also be retrieved independently from SATAN's documentation.

Additional sorting options in the "Reporting and Data Analysis" menu are the severity of the detected vulnerabilities and the type of security risk. Evaluating which vulnerabilities are severe and which are less so is certainly a very subjective matter and cannot actually be done without more exact knowledge of the situation. In general, all vulnerabilities that SATAN finds should be corrected. Naturally, however, vulnerabilities that enable a free root login are first on the priority list; this is where to start with the cleanup operation to correct the flaws.

Sorting by the type of vulnerability provides an overview of how frequently problems occur (see Figure 3-8). This list is particularly interesting. It may reveal gaps in the system administrator's knowledge. This can indicate system-related insecurities in an operating sytem. If the number of detected insecure hosts for a certain vulnerability corresponds to the number of hosts with a certain operating system version (for example, a detected "NFS export by portmapper" is almost always associated with a certain operating system version) then it's time for an upgrade!

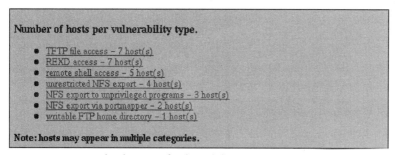

Figure 3-8. Sorting by the type of vulnerability

Figure 3-8 shows a typical result of a security audit; seven hosts reveal insecure TFTP daemons, and (coincidentally) seven hosts also permit program execution with *rexd*. It is conspicuous that five hosts allow free access for *remote shell*. This is very likely a workgroup distributed over five workstations. We would expect a similar number of open X Windows servers, which is not the case here. This suggests that the X Windows servers are well administered, but the underlying security mechanisms of the operating systems were not handled well.

Problems with NFS, i.e., export not restricted to certain clients, etc., occur relatively frequently in scanning complete networks, as is the case with the hosts in Figure 3-8.

Now let us return to the Data Analysis menu.

Under the heading "Host information" you can sort the acquired information from the database by services, operating system type, domain, subnetwork, or hostname. In addition to the number of hosts with the selected attributes, SATAN also displays how many of these are vulnerable. This permits a quick overview of how many hosts offer a given service, how many servers of a certain type are vulnerable, etc. This is an ideal feature for rapid report generation.

Sorting the data according to *trusted hosts* proves particularly interesting. Here you can determine which hosts share a trust relationship to which other hosts (trust relationships include importing filesystems, having active remote user logins, and trusting hosts other than DNS or NIS servers). In this way you can easily determine the particularly "important" hosts on the network, hosts that multiple other hosts trust. This is an easy way to identify workgroups that work on a central NFS server. If a host that many others trust is insecure, this also affects all clients! For security reasons such hosts must be handled with extra care.

However, even apart from security considerations, this representation provides a picture of the trust relationships between hosts on the network. Particularly in structures that evolved over time, or in open campus networks with little control over which hosts are connected how, this at least allows an overview of the status quo.

To print a report, use the **WWW** browser's print function for a hardcopy of the page that is currently displayed.

4

Scan Results and Countermeasures

In this chapter, we take a look at the different weaknesses SATAN tests for, and discuss some steps that can be taken to secure systems against attacks. This chapter is not meant to be a complete overview of network security issues; rather, it focuses on the insecurities that SATAN can detect as distributed. A basic knowledge of how UNIX network services like NFS and the remote shell work is assumed here; we explain *why* something is a security problem, but we do not explain in detail the inner workings of all the different network services.

What SATAN Tests

SATAN tests 13 different services that have weaknesses and frequent configuration errors that an attacker could exploit to access the system being tested. When SATAN detects security holes, it is important to understand why these hits present a security problem so that the system administrator can evaluate whether an insecure service really presents a problem. Certainly SATAN cannot know everything about the actual network architecture being tested. When SATAN detects a potential weakness, the system administrator must decide the following:

- Is the problem serious, or can we live with it?

- What will corrective measures cost? That is, the administrator must make a cost/benefit analysis and determine whether the investment pays off.

- Some network services are insecure per se, and the only way to assure a secure system is to terminate such services. Is it tenable for the organization, considering transition costs, to terminate a network service if termination is the only countermeasure?

SATAN can detect the following weaknesses:

- Writable FTP home directory

- WU-FTPD (older versions)

- NFS access by nonprivileged programs

- Filesystem export via portmapper

- Unrestricted NFS export

- Access to NIS maps

- Remote execution daemon (*rexd*)

- Unrestricted *rsh* access

- sendmail (older versions)

- TFTP access

- X.11 server

- Unrestricted modem access

- SATAN

Knowledge of these 13 security flaws is already built into SATAN as distributed. Extension to cover additional weaknesses is discussed in Chapter 5, *Extending and Adapting SATAN*.

Weaknesses and Countermeasures

Here we examine the individual problems in detail; we explain the weaknesses and provide tips for ameliorating or circumventing the problems. The "Additional Notes" section later in this chapter provides additional general instructions on several services.

Writable FTP Home Directory

FTP (File Transfer Protocol) is the name of both the transfer protocol and the program that implements this protocol. FTP enables file transfers between a client and a server. Normally this occurs with the client's own user ID on the server; however, an anonymous FTP server represents an exception where any user on the network has access. Anonymous FTP servers are quite popular on the Internet for making software or documents generally available.

If SATAN reports the weakness "writable FTP home directory," this means that the home directory of an anonymous FTP server is writable. This indicates that an attacker can use the FTP command *put* to create an *.rhosts* file to help gain access to the system, and that an intruder can use sendmail to execute arbitrary programs on the server after creating a *.forward* file! Furthermore, an intruder can change files in the directory tree of the anonymous FTP server. If the server's operating system is not a multiuser system (as with a PC under DOS, Windows, or NT, or a Macintosh), an intruder could modify arbitrary files on the server.

Correcting this weakness

To correct this problem, make sure that the home directory of the FTP server and all its subdirectories are owned by *root* and that anonymous users do not have write permission. This also applies to all files: no file and no directory should belong to the user *ftp*. The only exception should be a single directory, *~ftp/incoming*, which can be writable if you want to allow uploading of files. In this case you should grant write but not read permission for the *incoming* directory; this prevents your FTP server from becoming a public exchange for programs, images, etc. This also prevents anyone from modifying files on the server, even if an intruder does manage to obtain write permission as user *ftp* via some hole in the FTP daemon.

Anonymous FTP poses a multitude of potential problems caused by careless configuration. Here are some further suggestions:

- The user *ftp* must not have a login shell. In the file */etc/passwd*, change the shell to */bin/false*. Since the user *ftp* normally has no password, you would otherwise be providing a completely normal login without a password—you could hardly better encourage an attacker.

- If possible, you should use only statically linked commands for the directory *~ftp/bin*. Copy the files into the directory *~ftp/bin* and use no links. This precludes any modifications that an intruder might make to these programs from affecting normal users on the system. It also limits the number of system files (i.e., libraries) that need to be in the FTP tree.

- The directory *~ftp/etc* normally contains a *passwd* and a *group* file. These files are used by the UNIX *ls* command to display the owners and groups on an FTP *dir* command; make sure that these are not original copies of the */etc/passwd* or */etc/group* file! If that were the case, a cracker could simply download these files and run a password-cracking program on them locally. The *passwd* file needs to include only the user *root* and possibly any other users whose files reside on this server. The encrypted password field is not needed; the passwords must be deleted to prevent anyone from cracking them.

- No files and no directories should be owned by the user *ftp*. If they are, every user of the FTP server will be able to delete or, worse, change files at will.

WU-FTPD

WU-FTPD is a substitute for the standard FTP server delivered with a system. Developed at Washington University in St. Louis, Missouri, U.S.A., this program has won great popularity, especially among operators of anonymous FTP servers, because it provides significantly better logging and configuration features than the normal FTP daemon. In particular, WU-FTPD allows definition of access restrictions by classes to prevent overloading the server.

WU-FTPD is error-prone due to its sheer complexity. Older versions display *race conditions*, and bugs in the SITE EXEC command of FTP are also known. By exploiting the known errors, an attacker can gain root privileges on an FTP server. This works even if anonymous FTP is not activated!

Correcting this weakness

The simplest way to avoid security holes ensuing from software errors is to refrain from using the erroneous software ;-). If you do not particularly need the special features of WU-FTPD, it makes sense to use the standard FTP server of the operating system. It will likely have less functionality and be less complex, and thus be less prone to errors.

If this option is not viable, e.g., because the logging functions of WU-FTPD are required, then you must be sure to use the newest version, which has fixed these bugs (and hopefully not introduced new ones). The newest version can be obtained via anonymous FTP from the server *wuarchive.wustl.edu*.

You can also restrict access to your FTP server, for example, by using a TCP wrapper or a suitable router configuration, thereby allowing access only from trusted networks. However, this option is normally not available to operators of an anonymous FTP server, because by definition everyone should have access to the server.

NFS Access from Unprivileged Programs

NFS (the Network File System) is a widely used method of allowing multiple hosts to collectively use filesystems under UNIX. (While NFS is not really specific to UNIX, this is where it is most widely used.) A server can export files or directory trees to certain clients, and then clients can access these files or directories via the network like a local disk. NFS is most frequently used in workgroups that allow all workstations access to shared data.

In its standard form, the NFS protocol lacks strong authentication of clients. For an NFS client to access a network directory, it sends a corresponding request to the server. This request contains, among other things, the operation to be executed (write, read, etc.) and the user ID (UID) and group ID (GID) of the invoking user.

The UID and GID are only numbers in an IP packet; any user could write a program, e.g., a personal NFS client, that sends requests on behalf of arbitrary user IDs. This would allow the user read and write permission on the data of other users if this data is in an exported directory. Writing such a program is no Herculean feat; it simply requires knowledge of the C programming language and the corresponding system manual. In fact, crackers already have such programs, including the famed NFS shell.

To protect against such attacks, newer NFS versions enable testing from which port a request was started. If a request comes from a privileged port (< 1024), it is granted, while access requests from unprivileged ports (>= 1024) are denied. Since under UNIX only *root* can use privileged ports, this assures at least minimal security. However, after standard installation this test is normally disabled because it can cause problems with older client versions.

Obviously, this approach affords security only from users that have no *root* permissions on their computer (i.e., the NFS client). Nowadays this is a daring assumption, since users frequently administer their own systems on workstations. Additionally, this approach provides no security against users on PCs or Macs, for these computers do not employ the concept of privileged ports, so that any user can assign arbitrary ports in self-authored programs.

Correcting this weakness

It is extremely difficult to achieve security with NFS without significant intervention in the system. The solution would be to use authentication methods with a cryptographic approach such as Kerberos. However, few commercial sources produce such authentication methods, and in the heterogeneous system combinations that are usual today, it is hardly possible to introduce a vendor-specific solution.

At any rate, it does make sense to configure the NFS server and the mount daemon so that they accept requests only from privileged ports. Under SunOS 4, for example, start the mount daemon *without* the option −n and set the kernel variable *nfs_portmon*:

```
rpc.mountd
echo "nfs_portmon/W1" | adb -w /vmunix /dev/kmem
```

In other systems the mount daemon is started differently and the kernel variable might have a different (although similar) name.

In the section "Additional Notes" later in this chapter, you will find further suggestions about configuring NFS.

Filesystem Export via Portmapper

The portmapper (in BSD-related UNIX flavors) or *rpcbind* (in System V Release 4 variants) is the daemon that manages RPC services. It can be compared to *inetd*, which handles similar tasks for normal TCP or UDP/IP services. The portmapper (which always runs on port 111) handles mapping between RPC protocol names and RPC port numbers. As shown in Figure 4-1, when starting an RPC service, a client connects to the portmapper and asks for a particular service by a protocol number. The portmapper then tells the client on which port the service is running, and communication between the client and the server process then proceeds directly, without further intervention of the portmapper.

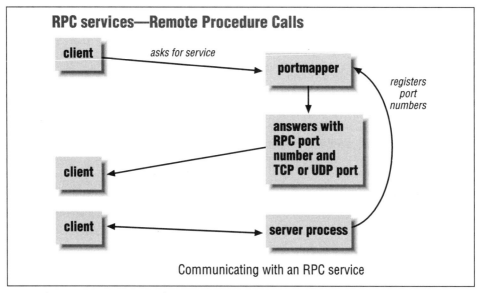

Figure 4-1. Communicating with an RPC service

For performance reasons, many NFS implementations do access control only while a client attempts to mount a filesystem. Host access control is usually absent for NFS requests such as *read* or *write*. The client sends a mount request to the server's mount daemon when a filesystem is to be mounted for the first time. On the basis of the *exports* table (usually in */etc/exports*, but for System V UNIX in */etc/dfs/dfstab*), *rpc.mountd* checks the permissions of the client and then assigns an NFS *file handle*, which is used for communication with the NFS daemon. Overall communication with the NFS daemon normally takes place without additional access control! An exception here is NFS access as superuser.

Now there are versions of *portmapper* and *rpcbind* that can function as a sort of relay station (see Figure 4-2). Instead of first asking the portmapper on which port the mount daemon is running in order to send a request to the portmapper, the request can be sent directly to the portmapper, with the request: "Forward this request to the *rpc.mountd*, and send me the reply from *rpc.mountd*." The simplicity of this approach for the programmer is counterbalanced by the fact that the mount daemon can no longer see which client sent the original request. For the mount daemon the request seems to have originated locally.

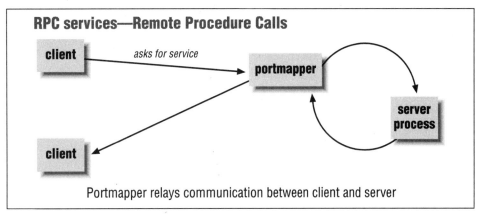

Figure 4-2. Communicating with an RPC service through portmapper

This nullifies any access control; if the server exports filesystems to an NIS netgroup of which it is itself a member, then any client can mount the filesystem.

Correcting this weakness

Use a portmapper version that does not forward requests. The vendor of the operating system you use should be able to provide such a version or to make patches available.

If it is not possible to replace such a forwarding portmapper, the risk can at least be reduced by exporting no filesystems to the server itself. However, the security achieved in this way is limited—the portmapper not only handles mount requests, but also provides other services that could be affected by this bug. Ideally, a computer that exhibits such behavior, where the behavior cannot be modified, should not be used as a server. At any rate, it has no business in any network that might in any way be a security risk.

Unrestricted NFS Export

SATAN reports this weakness if it finds one or more filesystems that are exported via NFS to the world, i.e., that any client can mount without restriction. For example, servers for diskless workstations often export completely and without restriction the filesystem in which the users have their home directories because this saves the administrator the trouble of adapting the *exports* file for each new work-station joining the workgroup. Because, as was shown above, user authentication for NFS is rather rudimentary in nature, this makes it easy for an intruder to read or modify files on the server or to achieve interactive access to the system by installing an *.rhosts* file.

Correcting this weakness

Make sure that for each export you enter an explicit list of clients or netgroups that may mount the respective filesystem. The entries are made in the file */etc/exports* or, under System V UNIX, in */etc/dfs/dfstab*.

Access to NIS Maps

The Network Information Service (NIS) permits networkwide access to administra-tive data. With a large number of workstations, this facilitates administration because user data can be maintained centrally on a server and all clients then have access to the current database. The data managed by NIS includes the following:

- */etc/passwd*, the password file
- */etc/group*, the file with the group assignments for users
- */etc/hosts*, the list of known hostnames and IP addresses

Similar to DNS, NIS databases are organized in domains.

The problem is that most NIS implementations afford absolutely no access con-trol. When a client queries an NIS server, this request includes the NIS domain name, the name of the database to be searched (also called a map, in NIS), and the key to be searched for. Thus anyone who knows the NIS domain name has full access to the above files. The NIS domain name is usually easy to guess and often identical to the DNS domain name. The *bootparam* service, which provides booting information for diskless workstations, frequently also kindly supplies the NIS domain name. This gives an attacker free access to the password file and enables downloading this file, running a cracking program on it, and trying the logins on a local workstation until access to the server is achieved.

Correcting this weakness

Several vendors offer the NIS server *ypserv* with access-control mechanisms. Here, a file (usually called *securenets*) contains entries defining which IP (sub)networks are permitted access to the server. This at least makes life more difficult for an attacker.

In the section "Additional Notes" later in this chapter, you will find further sugges-tions about configuring NIS.

Remote Execution Daemon (rexd)

rexd enables a user to remotely execute commands in the local environment. The corresponding command on the client is *on*, although this is not available on all UNIX systems.

Here, too, we are confronted with the lack of authentication. In addition to the text of the requested command, a request to execute a command via *rexd* also contains the UID and GID of the invoking user. By default, *rexd* trusts everything that is sent to it, so that an intruder with a self-authored frontend can use an arbitrary UID to execute programs on the server. The usual *rexd* daemons lack any access control mechanism.

Correcting this weakness

Normally, *rexd* is not used at all on most systems. The simplest solution to the problem therefore is to never start *rexd* in the first place. Suppress the start of *rexd* by commenting out the corresponding line in the file */etc/inetd.conf.* Then *inetd* must be restarted or induced to reread its configuration file by sending it a SIGHUP signal.

Some implementations of *rexd* can be configured so that they use a secure protocol. Under SunOS 4, e.g., *rexd* can be launched with the option -s, which enables authentication via a public-key procedure. If you need *rexd* and if the operating system permits it (and all clients support the secure protocol, which in heterogeneous environments is a daring assumption), you should choose this configuration.

Unrestricted rsh Access

Remote shell (*rsh*) access permits the interactive execution of arbitrary commands on a server. The client executing the *rsh* must belong to the *trusted hosts*. If SATAN detects unrestricted access to *rsh*, this means that the computer being tested trusts all other machines on the network. Thus any user can gain access without a password and execute programs.

Correcting this weakness

As a rule, unrestricted *rsh* (and thus *rlogin, rcp, rcmd,* and *rdist* as well) access occurs via erroneous configuration of the file */etc/hosts.equiv.* This file contains a list of trusted hosts, users, and netgroups, as well as those unworthy of trust. In any case, global wildcards must be deleted from this file. If you find a line that contains only a +, delete the line. A + alone means that any computer or user in the world can log in on your machine. Unfortunately, this is the default setting for some operating systems, e.g., SunOS 4.1.

The sequence of entries in *hosts.equiv* is important! During authentication of an *rsh* request, the user name, hostname, and NIS domain (when using NIS netgroups) are compared to entries in *hosts.equiv*. After the first match in *hosts.equiv*, processing stops, so it's important to put an entry denying access in front of an entry allowing access to the netgroup.

Assign system IDs such as *bin*, *daemon*, and *sys* a nonfunctional shell, e.g., */bin/false*. The operating system requires these IDs, but as a rule no user ever needs to log in under them. Even in the case of an erroneous configuration, this assignment prevents an intruder from achieving an interactive login with these IDs. Additionally, system IDs should be entered in */etc/ftpusers* so that no login is possible via FTP.

In the section "Additional Notes" later in this chapter, you will find further suggestions about configuring *rsh*.

sendmail

sendmail is a *Mail Transfer Agent* (MTA) that forwards email to other systems and receives email from other hosts or from local users. sendmail is so powerful that almost all mail servers on the Internet employ it. There are few alternatives that provide the same freedom of configuration. Since it is delivered with the operating system for almost all UNIX variants, the sendmail daemon is running on almost every UNIX host on the Internet, often in the less than correct configuration provided by the vendor.

Due to the complexity of sendmail and inadequate quality assurance, quite a number of errors found their way into this program. For example, almost all sendmail versions before February 1995 make errors in parsing strings, so that *newlines* or other control characters in addresses or command-line options produce undesirable results. Old releases of sendmail have numerous opportunities for attaining root privileges from a normal user account on the system, or even from a remote system.

Furthermore, sendmail permits sending mail to programs; the content of the mail is then processed by the receiving program. If sendmail executes the program with root privileges, as earlier versions did, an intruder has unsuspected opportunities.

Even without erroneous MTAs, the *Simple Mail Transfer Protocol*, SMTP, which is used on the Internet, presents several opportunities for spying. The SMTP commands VRFY (verify) and EXPN (expand) can be used to check the validity of a mail address and to expand a mail alias without actually sending mail. EXPN, in particular, provides the attacker with interesting data about the mail infrastructure, since it returns the hostnames on which the addressee is working, even if this would not be visible from the normal mail address.

Correcting this weakness

If your organization does not use SMTP mail, but X.400 or a proprietary mail system, then you should not launch sendmail at all. Comment out the corresponding lines in */etc/rc.local* or */etc/rc2.d/...*, depending on your operating system.

If you do use sendmail, use only the newest version; the current version as we go to press is 8.9. In the newer versions the known security holes have been plugged. sendmail can be downloaded via anonymous FTP from *ftp.sendmail.org* as well as from most other FTP servers on the Internet. The vendor of your operating system should also be able to provide you with a new version if you prefer not to compile your own copy.

The alias files for sendmail (usually */etc/aliases* or */usr/ucb/aliases*) delivered with your operating system often contain mail aliases that reference programs. An alias for the program *uudecode* is often included:

```
decode: "|/usr/bin/uudecode"
```

This pipes mail to the user *decode* through *uudecode*; *uudecode* decodes the mail and saves the resulting file where the sender wants it. Depending on the user ID under which sendmail runs, this can allow an attacker free write access to the filesystem.

Such aliases should be commented out or deleted, as they are almost never needed. In the above example a file transfer with FTP is just as comfortable as sending programs via email, and this option bears fewer security risks.

The use of EXPN and VRFY should be suppressed. In version 8 of sendmail, do this with the option Op in the sendmail configuration file, *sendmail.cf*:

```
# disallow EXPN and VRFY commands
Opnoexpn,novrfy
```

Thereafter, sendmail responds to EXPN and VRFY commands with an error message.

For use as a mail server on the Internet or on a firewall, you should consider using a frontend for sendmail like *smap*. *smap* is a very simple program, so it is easier to validate than sendmail. It runs in a *chroot* environment, so that even in the event of a mail catastrophe, the system cannot be mastered by an intruder. *smap* receives mail, checks it for correctness, and, after the mail passes all tests, stores it in a spool directory accessible to sendmail. sendmail then forwards the spooled mails. In this way there is never a direct connection between a client and sendmail, and *smap* can filter out mail bombs before they reach sendmail.

TFTP Access

TFTP, the *Trivial File Transfer Protocol*, is a sort of "FTP for the underprivileged." It works with UDP/IP and without any access control. This means that any networked user can read all files and upload or overwrite files wherever world write permissions are granted. A prerequisite for reading is that the name of the file to be read is known, since TFTP has no *dir* command like FTP has (though on some systems the command *get .* may get you the names of the files in the current directory).

TFTP is usually used to transfer configuration files and boot images. Diskless workstations and X terminals use it to load their operating systems; routers and hubs employ it to load their configuration from the network management system and sometimes also to download their operating system.

Correcting this weakness

In any case, TFTP must be launched with the option *secure*, thereby restricting access through TFTP to a certain directory tree. Change the line in */etc/inetd.conf* for the TFTP daemon to the following:

```
# Secure TFTP service
tftp   dgram   udp     wait    root    /usr/etc/in.tftpd       in.tftpd -s /
tftpboot
```

This example is for SunOS 4; on other operating systems, the name of the TFTP daemon might differ. The daemon normally resides in the directory */usr/etc*; change the path accordingly if the daemon is located elsewhere in your operating system. */tftpboot* is the usual name for the published *tftp* directory, but this can, of course, be changed to any other directory name. This makes good sense if */tftpboot* is located in the root filesystem, since otherwise the big bootimages, etc. crowd that filesystem.

Even with the *secure* option, any user can still read the files in the */tftpboot* directory. This is no problem for boot images, but for configuration files of active network components, an intruder can gain a healthy overview of the overall network infrastructure on the basis of the configuration for one or more routers. Therefore, pay special attention to the following:

Select the TFTP server carefully

Routers must not load their configuration from servers that are in endangered segments. In particular, the inner router of a perimeter LAN, a protective network of a firewall system, must never use a machine as a TFTP server that is itself in the perimeter LAN, i.e., accessible from the Internet and so endangered.

Carefully select the configuration

> Passwords for routers and other network components have no business in any configuration files that can be loaded via TFTP. Most modern routers (e.g., CISCO systems devices) allow storing the configuration in NVRAMs (nonvolatile RAMs); here—and nowhere else—is also the place to store passwords.

It is generally a good idea to store the complete configuration of routers that establish connections to the Internet or other external networks in the NVRAM if these routers and their TFTP servers are not equipped with interruption-free power supplies.* Otherwise, this can happen: after a power failure, routers and TFTP servers reboot. Because the TFTP server must first execute a filesystem check (*fsck*) before it can boot in multiuser mode, the routers, as they try to load their configuration, encounter a timeout, and thereby normally boot with a default configuration that is open in all directions.

X.11 Server

X Windows (X.11) is a graphical user interface with network capability. X.11 is client/server-based; the workstation or the X terminal functions as server and the application running on the host as client. The server provides as services its screen (via a window manager), keyboard, mouse, etc. and is practically remote-controlled by the application programs on the host. Due to the network capability, server and client need not be running on the same machine. This makes X Windows the ideal frontend for distributed computers: a user on an X terminal can open windows on other networked machines.

Depending on the vendor of the operating system, the X user interface is called OpenWindows, SINIX Windows, Open Desktop, etc., but the underlying technology is always X Windows.

If SATAN reports "unrestricted X server access," this means that a computer was detected that provides these services not just for specific hosts but for any host on the network. This means that anyone can utilize the X server on the respective computer at will. This implies the following:

- A user's keyboard entries on a terminal or workstation can be monitored, including passwords.

- Keyboard entries can be faked.

- Anything on the screen can be read.

- Arbitrary applications can be launched.

---

* If you have insufficient storage capacity, you should at least guarantee a bottom-line, emergency configuration that assures the functionality of the most important services.

An intruder can gain full control of such a computer.

Correcting this weakness

By default, X servers run with *host access control*; i.e., only select client computers are authorized to access the server. With the following command, the computer named **name** is authorized on the X server:

```
xhost +name
```

The following command disables access control, i.e., authorizes any computer:

```
xhost +
```

Such a line should be removed from any shell scripts and from the *Xsession* file.

Access control with *xhost* already offers rudimentary security. However, it suffers from the problem of all host-based control mechanisms, i.e., that any user on an authorized host can access the X server. Since we can assume that the host is a multiuser system, this works only if all users are trustworthy.

A better approach is user-based access control mechanisms such as the MIT-MAGIC-COOKIE-1 method. This method generates a string on the server that all clients must know, similar to a password, before they receive authorization to access the server. This password is stored in the file *.Xauthority* in the user's home directory that launches X Windows. The password is distributed to authorized users via *rsh* using the command *xauth*:

```
xauth extract -- $DISPLAY | rsh hostname xauth merge -
```

Under *xdm*, the X Display Manager, you can activate the MAGIC-COOKIE method by setting the entry for authorization in the file *xdm-config* to true:

```
DisplayManager*authorize: true
```

The following *.xserverrc* file serves as a small example of how this works without *xdm* if you launch X.11 with *xinit*:

```
# determine hostname
HOST=`hostname`
# The key must be some number that cannot be guessed.
# Generate a key (e.g., by using SATAN's md5-program).
randomkey=`(ps -l & netstat & ls -lR /dev &) 2>&1 | /usr/local/bin/md5`
# Enter the key in .Xauthority, once for IPC and once with hostname
xauth add ${HOST}/unix:0 . $randomkey
xauth add ${HOST}:0 . $randomkey
# Launch X server
exec /usr/bin/X11/X -auth $HOME/.Xauthority
```

This method makes an X server relatively secure from intruders. Since X.11 Release 5 we have additional (and better) authentication approaches that do not transmit the key over the network as plain text. However, encryption takes place with DES, and due to the export restrictions imposed by the U.S. government on this cryptographic algorithm, these authentication possibilities are not very widespread outside the U.S.A.

The documentation to your operating system indicates which of these access control mechanisms is supported for X.11. Whenever possible, employ a user-based mechanism.

Unrestricted Modem Access

If multiple users share a modem, for the sake of simplicity this modem is often connected to a UNIX workstation or terminal server and linked with a small server program so that the modem is easy to reach via telnet on a certain port. Users can then dial freely out of the company by entering the corresponding modem commands.

This is not a security problem in the normal sense: The security of the system itself is not compromised as long as the modem does not permit dial-in connections. However, an intruder can cause an unbelievably high telephone bill with your modem. Furthermore, you could have a problem if it turns out that a modem in your company was used for intrusions elsewhere.

Correcting this weakness

Such modems should not be connected to machines that can be reached freely from the Internet. If you use modems in this way, connect the computer behind a firewall. You should also use passwords to restrict the users who have access to the modem.

SATAN

Ironically, using SATAN can itself cause a small security hole.

SATAN uses its own HTTP server to provide the HTML pages for the input and output for the browser that is used. This server is protected. It accepts requests only if the requested URLs, or output pages, contain a password between server and client that has been established in advance. The password is a 16-byte-long quasi-random number. This authentication scheme is similar to the MIT-MAGIC-COOKIE-1 method used with X Windows.

Depending on the browser used, you might experience a data leak that lets the password trickle through to the outside. Thereby, possibly with the help of address spoofing, other clients can query SATAN's HTTP server and gain access to the data of the security audit. This would amount to publishing the weaknesses of all tested systems, plus the possibility of an attacker remotely executing commands on the system SATAN is running on!

This is possible because some WWW browsers disclose to the Web server the address from which they hyperlinked to the current URL. This is a feature that is particularly interesting for commercial providers of Web servers, because this allows them to analyze the user's behavior and the structure of information servers. If you branch from SATAN to an external Web server, whether via personal bookmarks or hyperlinks in the SATAN documentation, the WWW browser would disclose the secret password to the server, since it is part of the URL of the SATAN Web pages. You will find this feature in all versions of Netscape, among other browsers.

Correcting this weakness

Correcting this data leak is not easy unless you use a different client for WWW. However, SATAN (since version 1.1c) takes the following measures to prevent exploitation of this weakness:

- The random numbers used as passwords are recomputed with each start and cannot easily be guessed.

- Requests from computers other than the one on which SATAN is running are ignored.

- Requests for pages outside SATAN's HTML directory tree as well as requests for nonexistent pages or forms with unexpected data are not accepted.

- SATAN determines whether the browser you use has this data leak and displays this information. For technical reasons this does not occur at the start of the program, but only on following the second hyperlink. If this does occur, you should not access any external Web server as long as SATAN is running.

- If the HTTP server receives an illegal request that contains the correct password, it assumes that the security has been compromised. SATAN then displays a warning and immediately terminates.

This security problem is certainly less critical than other system weaknesses detected by SATAN. Exploiting this weakness would require that an attacker run a Web server, that you use this Web server at least once, and—for the attacker to make use of the password—that the computer on which SATAN is running can be reached directly.

Nevertheless, this does reveal two fundamental points:

- Writing a secure program is not a trivial matter. The route is full of traps and potential holes that even experts like the authors of SATAN can readily miss.

- The data leak occurs not only when working with SATAN but also each time a Web browser with this feature accesses external servers. This is a perfect example of how information about the structure of your local network can leak outside in the Internet despite the use of the most modern firewall mechanisms. Consider the example of a large company that operates internal Web servers (an intranet) connected via firewall with proxy servers that are connected to the Internet: Over time the operator of a Web server on the Internet can achieve a precise overview of which internal servers exist and which URLs are available there. While this information is not adequate to prepare an intrusion, an outsider can nevertheless accumulate information that is otherwise not public.

How Critical Are the Detected Holes?

Not all weaknesses that SATAN finds necessarily lead to an intrusion. Depending on the nature of the network, which computers are connected to the network, and which users work on which computers, priority can be assigned to each problem.

The detected security holes can be divided into two categories:

Weaknesses that can be exploited only with custom-tailored clients
   These include NFS export via portmapper, using custom clients to mount filesystems exported with NFS, and monitoring keyboard input, etc., via accessible X.11 servers. To exploit these holes, a cracker must have the expert knowledge to program these clients and must be able to compile them on a host on the network; i.e., a cracker needs either access to a development system, or to precompiled clients (for example from the Internet) to install them on the target system.

Security holes that can be exploited with shell commands,* or with standard system utilities
   Here it suffices if the hacker has any account on some host on the network. This category covers all other holes that SATAN can detect.

In closed environments† the weaknesses in the first category can often be handled with lower priority. This is especially true for a diskless workstation configuration, where introducing private custom software is at least encumbered if not prevented. This scenario occurs often in nontechnical departments in insurance, banking, and commercial organizations. On the other hand, holes that can be exploited with shell commands must be plugged immediately.

---

* Or the corresponding equivalents under MS-DOS or other operating systems.

† Networks that are not freely accessible and in which users work with strictly defined applications and have no development system available.

In open networks, by contrast, both categories prove equally critical, and the weaknesses need to be corrected promptly. This applies especially for hosts that are accessible from public networks such as the Internet—in such cases, action must be taken immediately.

This by no means implies that the weaknesses designated here as less critical should not be corrected or that there is no urgency to do so. The closed-environment argument that "my users can't program anyway!" is not tenable. These users have friends who can program, or who from the comfort of their homes can retrieve finished programs from cracker archives or the Internet. Such an intrusion is particularly serious in closed networks because it usually catches the system administrator off guard. Furthermore, a closed network is often not as isolated as its operators believe. Can you be sure that none of your users is hiding a modem in a desk drawer?

Furthermore, a problem might simply fend off all efforts to correct it. Problems due to erroneous configuration or insufficient restriction are easy to correct. However, if a security hole reported by SATAN demands an operating system update or the installation of patches, you might encounter dependencies on installed application programs that seriously delay or block the required update.

In such a case, the only damage control is a comprehensive security concept to quickly detect any exploitation of a known weakness and enable immediate countermeasures. Chapter 7, *Beyond SATAN*, presents more details on such a security concept. However, this cannot and should not substitute for correcting a security flaw!

Additional Notes

Some additional notes for configuring NFS, NIS, and *rlogin* or *rsh* should prove helpful, since this is where most erroneous configurations seem to occur, and because security lapses in these services are also easiest for a cracker to detect and exploit.

NFS

If possible, directories should be exported as read-only (i.e., write-protected). Although this does not prevent the theft of data, it at least protects against a hacker modifying existing files. System directories, if they indeed must be exported, absolutely must be tagged read-only so that an intruder cannot modify any system files.

Root access to NFS filesystems should generally be avoided. It is a trivial matter to attain root permissions on an NFS server if root access by clients is enabled. Fortunately, the default setting does not permit root access; root access must be explicitly enabled on the server with the option `root=clientname` in */etc/exports*, or, on System V, */etc/dfs/dfstab*. Determine which clients really need root access.

NFS generally has no business on firewalls or on hosts freely accessible from the Internet, unless particularly secure variants of NFS are employed. The corresponding daemons (*nfsd*, *rpc.mountd*) should not be started; ideally the ports used by the portmapper and by the NFS daemon should be completely locked in the router (portmapper: port 111, NFS: port 2049). If NFS mounts are absolutely necessary—and you are absolutely sure you know what you are doing—a wrapper can restrict access. Furthermore, such a wrapper provides better logging features than the portmapper that is delivered with the operating system. Such a wrapper can be downloaded via anonymous FTP from *ftp.win.tue.nl*, directory */pub/security*. Nevertheless, a wrapper alone cannot provide full security.

NIS

Regarding security aspects, NIS is really suitable only for use in isolated workgroups; in open networks NIS tempts hackers with too many vulnerabilities. Certainly its greatest flaw (described in the section "Access to NIS Maps" earlier in this chapter) is the ability to read the NIS maps (and thus the password file as well). In addition, it lacks server authentication features. NIS clients find their server by sending a broadcast into the network and believing anyone who responds. Although some NIS implementations allow the restriction of which clients on NIS servers may work on privileged ports (the *secure* option of *ypbind*, *ypbind –s*), this offers little protection. The problem is the same as with NFS.

We frequently encounter the advice that choosing an NIS domain name that cannot be guessed, such as a random string, protects against unauthorized access. While at first glance this might seem credible—no NIS domain name means no access to the NIS server—a closer look shows that this is humbug. The NIS domain name must be known to all clients and is thus also known to all users. A secret that everyone knows is no secret.

Due to these weaknesses, especially since NIS enables obtaining the global *passwd* file, when using NIS it becomes even more important to emphasize the quality of passwords. It is a well-known problem that users tend to choose easy-to-guess passwords because they are easy to remember. Password cracking programs like *crack* quickly uncover passwords. It makes sense to conduct a regular check of the *passwd* file with a tool like *crack* to detect such easy-prey passwords so that they can be changed. There are also */bin/passwd* programs that detect and reject trivial passwords, thus forcing users to select more secure passwords.

NIS+, the successor to NIS, provides better security mechanisms, but it is not supported by all vendors. If you work in a system environment in which all operating systems support NIS+ and you currently use NIS, you should upgrade to NIS+.

NIS must not run on any computer that is accessible from the Internet.

rsh, rcp, rlogin, etc.

In addition to the computers and users that are granted password-free authorization in *hosts.equiv*, by means of the file *.rhosts* users can also grant access to their login to all or to specified users on remote systems via the "r-services" *rlogin*, *rcp*, *rsh*, etc.

It is generally not a good idea to use *.rhosts* files. They provide an attacker who reads them valuable information about other hosts from which access is possible. Since *.rhosts* files often exist mutually, the attacker also gains a list of additional worthwhile targets. *.rhosts* files under administrative logins such as root should be deleted. Although it requires more effort for the administrator to enter a password on each login, the security gains are considerable. Even normal users should not use *.rhosts* files. If you choose to use them anyway, at least be sure that only the owner has read and write permissions.

Avoid *.rhosts* files on filesystems exported via NFS; you cannot always assure that they are read/write only for the owner, even if the permissions seem to be clear (see the section on NFS earlier in this chapter).

A general problem in the authentication of authorized users via *.rhosts* is that it is based on hostnames. It assumes that DNS (or NIS) returns correct answers to a query for the hostname of a client. This assumption might be justified in an isolated local network, but the Internet is a different ball game. DNS servers themselves can be attacked, and every operator of a DNS server can provide falsified data to you, trying to bypass hostname-based authentication (see Chapter 7, *Beyond SATAN*, for a more detailed description of this problem). If you strive for optimal security, you must dispense with *hosts.equiv* and *.rhosts* files.

Summary

The 13 weaknesses that SATAN can detect certainly represent the most frequent erroneous configurations and the most frequent holes used for attacks. When such a weakness is discovered, it needs to be rectified at once. SATAN itself is not a cracker tool employed for intrusion; however, since it is so easy to use and fun to work with, it does seduce some folks to play around with it—and then it becomes tempting to try out some detected weakness just once.

Abide by the motto "SATAN: Run it before your users do!"

5

Extending and Adapting SATAN

Why Extend SATAN?

One of SATAN's great strengths is its easy extensibility, a result of its modular architecture. You can extend SATAN with rules to identify new systems or to scan local vulnerabilities (e.g., a proprietary mail system, database servers, etc.) that are not covered as part of the basic "plug-and-play" SATAN.

In the course of a normal test, there is certainly no need to modify SATAN. For advanced users, SATAN's extensibility offers broad and interesting options that include a fully automated security audit of the network, completely adapted to local requirements. This proves particularly advantageous in networks with many proprietary systems, because SATAN, as delivered, is configured for mainstream operating systems. If you employ less popular variants of operating systems or have your own client/server applications, SATAN should be customized.

To make custom extensions, you should be familiar with shell programming and Perl. You need not be a UNIX guru, but a basic knowledge of regular expressions and Perl is necessary to understand the syntax of the rules for evaluations. If you want to link your own tools to test specific network services, these can be written in any programming language (or employ existing system commands). A small program must start the tools and format their output in a prescribed manner to match SATAN's database record format.

We first need to make a small excursion into SATAN's architecture in order to understand how SATAN acquires its testing goals and how its scans are evaluated. Then three examples show how to expand SATAN. If you are looking for a fast solution and can do without the details, proceed directly to the examples.

SATAN's Architecture

SATAN consists of three primary modules—the policy engine, the target acquisition engine, and the data acquisition engine—and a governing control program, the inference engine. These modules contain no hard-wired knowledge about networks, protocols, or operating systems; what is to be done, the scheduling of scans, and the meaning of scan results are all specified in the configuration file and in rules (in the directory *~satan/rules*). Thus, by editing the rules or the configuration file, you can extend and adapt SATAN to your own requirements without meddling with SATAN's code.

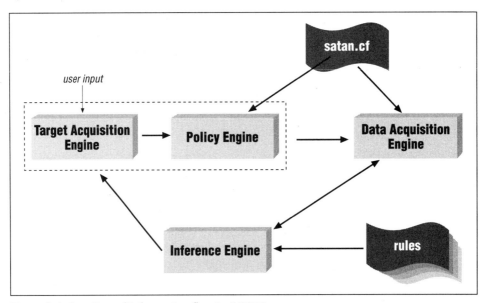

Figure 5-1. Overview of information flow in SATAN

In the following sections we examine the individual modules more closely.

Modules

The *policy engine (~satan/perl/policy.pl)* determines which hosts can be targets of a test and at what level (light, normal, or heavy) the test is to be conducted. The policy engine is controlled by the configuration file *~satan/config/satan.cf,* which specifies which hosts, Internet domains, or (sub)nets are to be excluded from testing. Default values for scan severity are also specified in this file.

The *target acquisition engine (~satan/perl/targets.pl)* generates a list of targets for testing. Targets can be individual hosts or complete subnetworks. In the latter case, the engine expands the network addresses to host addresses and adds to the list of targets any addresses that are occupied, i.e., any address for a real host. To determine which addresses are actually used, SATAN launches the tool *~satan/bin/ fping*, which sends a *ping* to each address and outputs a list of responding hosts. If *ping* does not work in the network, e.g., because filtering routers block the ICMP protocol, SATAN can be configured to skip the *ping* test and to assume that all hosts are alive. That is, it accepts all addresses as targets. After completing the list, SATAN also records the scanning severity for each host. This data, along with targets that must be removed from the list because they cannot be scanned, is taken from the policy engine.

The input for the target acquisition engine can be obtained either from the user via the HTML interface (from the input field for which hosts or networks are to be tested) or from the inference engine, which can generate new targets at any time during a scan. It is important that potential targets appear in the list only once; otherwise, (direct or indirect) mutual dependencies among hosts, e.g., between two hosts that are mutually *trusted hosts*, could create an infinite loop. Therefore SATAN checks the entries for redundancy to avoid this case.

Actual scanning occurs through the data acquisition engine. For each target and according to the specifications in *~satan/config/satan.cf*, SATAN launches a tool that strives to find exactly one certain security hole, or one piece of information on the service currently being tested. The tools reside in the directory *~satan/bin*; the filenames all end in *.satan*. This is only a convention, but does help to provide an overview. In their command lines, the tools accept as an argument the name of the target host; their output must be in the standardized SATAN database record format described in the section "SATAN's Database Record Format" later in this chapter.

The inference engine interprets the data collected by the tools. Actually, it encompasses six small automata that are controlled by user-configured rules in the directory *~satan/rules*.

Rules

The rules for the inference engine concentrate the actual knowledge of network services and their vulnerabilities. A scan of all TCP/IP or UDP/IP ports returns a landslide of data. The tasks of SATAN's six rule engines are to raise the relevance density of this data by suppressing irrelevant data, evaluate the remaining interesting data, and transform it to a form that is readable by humans. The rules are stored in six files, corresponding to the six small automata.

Drop

The *drop* file specifies which detected vulnerabilities and other information should be ignored. SATAN cannot determine which data returned by its tools represents real security holes and which is negligible; this interpretation must be done by humans. It is normal, for example, to export CD-ROMs via NFS freely so that any staff member can access them, even without a local CD-ROM drive. In such a case, the tool *showmount.satan* would detect all such exports as security problems and sound the alarm.

However, in this special case, free NFS export is not a problem because a CD-ROM is read-only: thus the usual NFS attacks fail. Therefore, by default, an exported CD-ROM drive (normally mounted under */cdrom* on the server) is listed in the drop rule:

```
# Don't complain about /cdrom being exported to the world.
#
$text =~ /exports \/cdrom/i
```

The drop rules prove especially helpful when certain frequent false alarms need to be silenced. In this way, you can prevent important messages from getting lost in a deluge of other text.

The entries in *~satan/rules/drop* are Perl statements. All SATAN functions, as well as the global variables `$target` (the target system) and `$text` (the text that is output when a respective vulnerability is found) can be used here. The example tests whether `$text` contains **exports /cdrom** (case-insensitive).

Facts

In the *facts* rules, security-relevant data is extracted from text messages from the tools and especially from the banners of services like telnet, SMTP, FTP, etc. These rules contain much of the knowledge of possible vulnerabilities. The format of *~satan/rules/facts* is quite simple: in each line, the first field contains a Perl expression that is applied to the text message, and in the second field (delimited from the first field by a tabulator) is a SATAN database entry that contains the most significant derived data in short form. The following example is for the WU-FTP daemon:

```
# 220 wuarchive.wustl.edu FTP server (Version wu-2.4(1) Mon
/ftp.*\(version wu-2.([0-9]+)/i && $1 < 4 \
$target|assert|a|rs|ANY@$target|ANY@$target|FTP vulnerabilities|wuftp pre 2.4
```

The SATAN database record format used here is also the output format for the tools that are launched by the *data acquisition* module.

Host type

The file *~satan/rules/hosttype* contains the rules that let SATAN identify the operating system of a scanned host. As with the *facts*, the banners for the services telnet, FTP, and SMTP are evaluated. The structure of these rules is similar to that of *facts*; each line begins with a regular expression, and if this expression applied to a banner returns "true," then the text of the second field of the rule is output. This text identifies, in human-readable form, the type of computer hardware and operating system. If the second field is omitted, then by default the first regular Perl expression in the first field is output.

Because the banners of various versions of the same operating system can vary greatly, the individual identification rules are divided into classes. These classes permit clear rough classification of systems by vendor or by the flavor of the operating system used.

The following example shows an entry for UNIX System V:

```
CLASS SYSTEM V
UNKNOWN && /(System V) Release ([.0-9]+)/ "$1.$2"
UNKNOWN && /(System V[.0-9]*)/
```

UNKNOWN is set by default if no further information is available on a host. Although DNS contains a HINFO record that includes information in a standardized format on the hardware and OS used, these records are not often found, and the information therein is of dubious reliability. For this reason SATAN finds this information, but does not evaluate it to determine the type of system.

The file *hosttype* needs to be extended if systems in the scanned network are not (sufficiently) identified by SATAN.

Services

Here the cryptic messages of the SATAN tools concerning detected network services are transformed to a form readable by humans. The *services* rules only serve to format the generated reports and evaluations in a comprehensible way; the output of these rules is not processed further.

The structure is similar to the above rules; the first field is a Perl expression, and, when applied to the output of the tools, if it returns true, then the second field is output. An optional third field specifies the host for which this service is offered; if this field is omitted, by default the current host being tested is assumed.

For example, a Web server running on a nonprivileged port (a frequent occurrence, especially on port 8080) is easy to detect after the following transformation:

```
/<title>/i && $service ne "http"          WWW (nonstandard port)
```

This rule assumes that the Web server sends a standard HTML document with a document title (the HTML statement `<title>`). The variable `$service` stands for the network service (RPC-based or normal) that is currently being scanned. The content of `$service` is the official protocol designation of the service as it appears in */etc/services* or, for RPC services, in */etc/rpc*.

Todo

As the name implies, this file specifies what to do next if there are dependencies between services or if the presence of a certain service suggests the execution of a specific scan. A *todo* rule is structured as follows:

```
expression (tab) target tool options
```

The first field contains a logical expression; if it is true, the program *tool* is launched with the following command line:

```
tool options target
```

For example, testing whether a TFTP server allows unrestricted read access or even write access is started with the following rule:

```
$service eq "tftp"                   $target "tftp.satan"
```

The command `$target tftp.satan` is executed only if the service TFTP is actually provided by a server. This prevents the long wait for a timeout that would result otherwise.

Likewise, machine-specific rules can be defined here. The most frequent examples of machine-specific rules are standard logins that some vendors have set up for their operating systems, e.g., *guest* or *service*. The expression in this case corresponds to the host's type:

```
$untrusted_host && /IRIX/           $target "rsh.satan" "-u guest"
```

This example tests for the existence of the login *guest* without password protection on hosts known to be running the IRIX operating system. Here, SATAN attempts to start a remote shell under the user ID *guest*—however, this occurs only if the host on which SATAN is running has not been entered in *.rhosts*, */etc/hosts.equiv*, or similar files on the target host, i.e., if the variable `$untrusted_host` is set. Without this restriction *rsh* would start in any case, and SATAN would report a vulnerability whether or not it really exists.

Trust

The rules for recognizing trust relationships between hosts are structured similarly to those for identifying the host type or services and have the following general format:

```
condition (tab) plaintext
```

These rules translate the cryptic messages from the SATAN databases to a form readable by humans. In Version 1 of SATAN, the recognition of trust relationships, that is, of dependencies between hosts, is still quite rudimentary. The following cases are recognized:

- *root* login from another host

- User login, (i.e., under a normal user ID) from another host

- NFS exports

- NIS/yellow pages server

- Boot clients

- DNS server

For recognizing network structures, the most interesting aspects are usually not the logins but dependencies in directory services such as NIS and DNS or file services such as NFS.

SATAN's Database Record Format

SATAN's database record format (see Figure 5-2) provides a uniform output format for all tools that are used. This enables automatic evaluation of the resulting data.

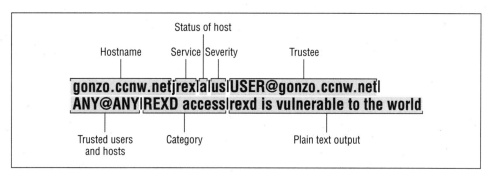

Figure 5-2. SATAN database record format

The file format consists of the following eight[*] fields delimited by vertical bars (|):

- The target of the test is a hostname with or without a domain, or the IP address of the target host if the name cannot be determined.

- The second field contains the name of the executed tool that returned the data, or, if one tool scans several services (e.g., *rpcinfo*, whose output covers

---

[*] SATAN documentation erroneously specifies seven fields.

all running RPC services), the name of the tested service. The name of the service is extracted from the file */etc/services* or */etc/rpc.*

- Next we have the status of the target host, with the following coding:

  a Available. The target host is accessible via the network.

  u Unavailable. This normally indicates that a timeout was encountered during probing.

  b Bad. The hostname could not be resolved to an IP address, or some other problem arose, so that SATAN could do nothing with the name or the address of the host.

  x Additional testing is necessary (not yet implemented).

- The fourth field is the severity of the security vulnerability. SATAN distinguishes among the following severities:

  rs Root shell. It is possible to obtain root permissions.

  us User shell. An attacker can log in as a normal, unprivileged user.

  ns Nobody shell. A login as user "nobody" is possible.

  uw User write. Write permission can be obtained under any user ID.

  nr Nobody read. Read access to data (as user "nobody") is enabled.

  x Additional testing is necessary (not yet implemented).

- The next field specifies objects, i.e., users or filesystems, that extend particular trust to other hosts. They are represented in the form "user@host" or "filesystem@host". Trust as used in this field is a flexible term. It means that the specified object is provided to other hosts and that the users or hosts specified in the next field can use a service (login, NFS, etc.).

- The users and hosts that are trusted (formatted like the fifth field) are entered in the sixth field. These could be active logged-in sessions initiated from the hosts specified here, or NFS clients. ANY indicates that any user or host has access to the trusting object.

- The next field contains the collective term for the detected vulnerability or the service name if the record does not identify a vulnerability. SATAN uses the text entered here to sort the records in the data analysis menu according to vulnerabilities and to find the corresponding HTML page with the documentation for the vulnerability so that an appropriate hyperlink can be generated.

- The final field describes the record in plain text for output on screen.

All tools launched by SATAN must save their results in this format. If a field is omitted, this means that no further statement can be made about the host or service to be tested, as in the following examples:

```
ab4u204.some.domain|netbios-ns|a|x||||offers netbios-ns
```

The host *ab4u204* provides NetBIOS name services. Because further tests of Net-BIOS have not been implemented in SATAN, nothing else can be added.

```
ab2w135.some.domain|showmount|a|x|/@ab2w135.some.domain|root@ANY|
unrestricted NFS export|exports / to everyone
```

The tool *showmount.satan* has detected that *ab2w135.some.domain* exports its root filesystem per NFS to everyone; the user *root* on any arbitrary host can mount "/". From the collective term "unrestricted NFS export," SATAN constructs a hyperlink that points to the output HTML page *~/satan/html/tutorials/vulnerability/ unrestricted_NFS_export.html*. There a user can find additional notes on the problem and tips for correction.

SATAN's Configuration File (satan.cf)

The configuration file *satan.cf* centrally regulates all of SATAN's activities. All tools and scripts that comprise SATAN have access to the variables that are set here. *satan.cf* is nothing more than another Perl script that is launched at the start of a SATAN session. However, even without knowledge of Perl, it is easy to understand and modify because it is well commented and contains no actual source code, but only assignments to various variables and structures.

Most entries in *satan.cf* can be modified via the configuration menu, and that approach is preferred as a matter of convenience for setting variables in normal operation. However, some settings are possible only in the configuration file. In our treatment here, we emphasize the variables that cannot be modified in the configuration menu. A complete overview of all the variables and their default settings in *satan.cf* can be found in Table 5-1.

Table 5-1. satan.cf Variables and Default Settings

Variable Name	Default Value	Explanation
$satan_data	"satan_data"	The default database name SATAN uses.
$attack_level	0	The severity of a probe. Default is 0 ("light").
@light	'dns.satan', 'rpc.satan', 'showmount.satan?'	The tools that are executed when a light probe is run. Defaults are checking the DNS, checking for RPC services and NFS exports (if NFS is available).

Table 5-1. satan.cf Variables and Default Settings (continued)

Variable Name	Default Value	Explanation
@normal	@light, 'finger.satan', 'tcpscan.satan 70,80,ftp,tel-net,smtp,nntp,uucp,6000', 'udpscan.satan 53,177', 'rusers.satan?', 'boot.satan?', 'yp-chk.satan?'	The tools that are executed when a normal probe is run. Defaults are all the tools of a light probe, finger, scanning frequently used TCP and UDP ports, and—if these services are offered on the computer being audited—checking rusers, bootparam and yp services.
@heavy	@normal, $heavy_tcp_scan = 'tcp-scan.satan 1-9999', $heavy_udp_scan = 'udp-scan.satan 1-2050,32767-33500', '*?'	The tools that are executed when a heavy probe is run. Defaults are all the tools of a normal probe, scanning most of the TCP and UDP ports of the system and running all the tools that have not been used so far.
$status_file	"status_file"	Where SATAN keeps its status information.
$short_timeout	10	Timeout value (short).
$med_timeout	20	Timeout value (medium).
$long_timeout	60	Timeout value (long).
%timeouts	'nfs-chk.satan', 120, $heavy_tcp_scan, 120, $heavy_udp_scan, 120,	More timeout values for those tools that take a bit longer to run.
$timeout_kill	9	The signal to use to kill a tool that has reached the timeout limit.
$max_proximity_level	0	How far out from the original target is probed. Default: 0, meaning we probe only the original target.
$proximity_descent	1	Amount by which the probe level is decreased when the proximity level changes.
$sub_zero_proximity	0	Should the probing go on when the attack level goes below 0? Default is 0 (stop).
$attack_proximate_subnets	0	Attack subnets or just the target? 0 means probe only the target computer.
$untrusted_host	0	Is the computer SATAN runs on an untrusted host? 0 means no, this computer might appear in .rhosts-files and the like.

Table 5-1. satan.cf Variables and Default Settings (continued)

Variable Name	Default Value	Explanation
`$only_attack_these`	""	Attack only these domains or networks.
`$dont_attack_these`	""	Never attack the domains or networks that appear here.
`$dont_use_nslookup`	0	Is DNS unavailable? 0 means no (i.e., DNS works), 1 means yes.
`$dont_use_ping`	0	Is ICMP broken? 0 means no, 1 means yes.

The default value for the severity of a probe is specified in the variable `$attack_level`. The valid values are 0 (light), 1 (normal), and 2 (heavy). Which actions SATAN executes on which attack level are specified by assignment of the corresponding tool name to the structures light, normal, and heavy:

```
# Default attack level (0=light, 1=normal, 2=heavy).
$attack_level = 2;
# Probes by attack level.
#
@light = (
        'dns.satan',
        'rpc.satan',
        'showmount.satan?',
        );
```

The example shows that a light scan executes the tools *dns.satan*, *rpc.satan*, and *showmount.satan*. Thus the domain name service is queried for the target host, the command `rpcinfo -p <target>` is executed to find the running RPC services, and the command `showmount` is executed to detect NFS exports.

```
@normal = (
        @light,
        'finger.satan',
        'tcpscan.satan 70,80,ftp,telnet,smtp,nntp,uucp,6000',
        'udpscan.satan 53,177',
        'rusers.satan?',
        'boot.satan?',
        'yp-chk.satan?',
        );
```

A normal scan tests whether the *finger* service is running, whether the corresponding daemons are running, for several common services such as gopher (port 70) and WWW (port 80), and runs several tests to extract additional information from the services *rusers* and *bootparam* and from the *yellow-pages*, and because of the following line, all probes normally carried out by a light scan are run:

```
@light,
```

This line inserts the contents of the array *light* in the list of probes for the normal scan.

```
@heavy = (
        @normal,
        $heavy_tcp_scan = 'tcpscan.satan 1-9999',
        $heavy_udp_scan = 'udpscan.satan 1-2050,32767-33500',
        '*?',
        );
```

The list of actions for a heavy scan is structured analogously; in addition to all actions assigned to the normal scan, additional TCP and UDP ports are probed for running daemons.

The "?" after the last tool name has a special meaning; it causes the corresponding tool to be executed only if a condition is fulfilled (usually, the condition is that a certain daemon is running). This prevents long waits for timeouts. For example, tools that probe RPC services (e.g., *rusers.satan* and *yp-chk.satan*) are launched only if the corresponding server is running on the target host. The conditions governing when a tool is to be launched are specified in the *todo* rules.

The line "*?" in the heavy scan starts all remaining tools that appear in the *todo* rules and have not been named yet.

Note that in the default configuration SATAN does not probe all possible ports of the TCP or UDP protocols, but only ports 1 to 9999 for TCP and 1 to 2050 and 32767 to 33500 for UDP. For efficiency reasons, these constraints restrict the probes to only those ports where experience has shown that most services are offered. A complete scan would have to cover all ports from 1 to 65,535, and would take significantly longer.

While the values for timeouts can be set more easily via the configuration menu, exceptions can be specified only in the configuration file. Some of SATAN's tools simply take longer, especially if the scanned server is quite busy.

```
# Some tools need more time, as specified in the timeouts array.
#
%timeouts = (
        'nfs-chk.satan', 120,
        $heavy_tcp_scan, 120,
        $heavy_udp_scan, 120,
        );
```

Here we could also insert the tools *yp-chk.satan* and *ypbind.satan*, because a busy NIS server might take somewhat longer to reply to the many queries that these tools generate.

Likewise the name of the status file that SATAN uses to determine which tools were launched when can be set only in the configuration file, or, alternatively, via the command line. Normally this name would be changed only for automatic SATAN runs so that each instance of SATAN writes to its own file.

```
# status file; keeps track of what SATAN is doing.
$status_file = "status_file";
```

Examples

The three following examples demonstrate ways in which SATAN can be expanded to meet the needs of your environment.

Recognizing a New Operating System

If a network includes numerous hosts that SATAN in standard configuration does not identify, the output in the data analysis menu will be less productive, because most hosts appear as "unknown hosttype." This situation can be improved by entering a new rule in the file *~satan/rules/hosttype*.

First search the banners of telnet, FTP, or SMTP for a string that uniquely identifies the new system. For example, SCO Openserver 5 can be identified by extending *CLASS other*:

```
CLASS other
/SCO Openserver\(TM\) Release ([0-9])/     "SCO Openserver $1"
```

The following is an example that is not a host in the usual sense (for a CISCO router):

```
CLASS other
/User Access Verification/          "CISCO Router"
```

New classes can also be defined as needed.

Unfortunately, further classifying System V hosts by vendor is usually difficult because these systems normally report only the System V release status rather than a vendor-specific string. Likewise some hosts (e.g., some Pyramid models) cannot be identified by their messages alone.

Naturally, identifying an operating system from its banner message assumes that this banner has not been modified. If a host employs daemons other than the standard ones delivered with the operating system, e.g., a self-ported sendmail version, the WU-FTPD, or special firewall software, recognition can fail. However, even then identification is sometimes possible by triggering the software that is used. For example, the following identifies a firewall system that uses this software:

```
CLASS other
/netsafe/i       "NetSafe-Galaxy Firewall System (SINIX / RM)"
```

This enables conclusions about the host and the operating system.

Identifying a Proprietary Service

Similar to identifying new hosts and operating systems, new services can be identified with an unambiguous entry in the file *~satan/rules/services*. The identification string should be selected carefully to avoid erroneous identification, hence it should be a long character string with character combinations that certainly would not appear elsewhere in this form.

To identify the backup server *yBackup* (proprietary software), for example, you could use the following entry:

```
/yBackup (\d+)/          "yBackup service Version $1"
```

The following string would identify a POP (Post Office Protocol) mail server:

```
/Pop /i          "POP server"
```

As with identifying the host type, 100% identification of a service is not always possible. Consider the standard entry for a Web server running on a nonstandard port:

```
/<title>/i && $service ne "http"      WWW (nonstandard port)
```

Here the Web server is identified because every document that it returns contains the HTML statement `<title>`. However, this is the case only if the pages of this server were properly programmed.

Integrating New Scans

Testing for vulnerabilities that off-the-shelf SATAN cannot detect is one of the most interesting activities. This simply requires writing a program to scan for a certain vulnerability, and a Perl script that SATAN can invoke and that provides output in a certain format. This required adherence to a common output format allows SATAN to apply the above general rules after the scan.

As an example to serve as a pattern for your own scripts, we will develop a script that tests a Windows NT server for whether it allows unrestricted mounting of file regions (shares). In terms of functionality and security aspects, this amounts to a UNIX server that exports a directory tree via NFS without restrictions. Naturally the technical details are different; Windows networks employ the SMB (Server Message Block) protocol rather than NFS.

First you need to find a tool that implements the SMB protocol in order to access an NT server at all. To avoid the temptation of programming an SMB client yourself (that could be the subject of a dedicated book), we will resort to SAMBA. Written by Andrew Tridgell, SAMBA is available via anonymous FTP from *nimbus.anu.edu.au* in the directory */pub/tridge/samba*. It is an excellent SMB server and client implementation for UNIX.

SAMBA's SMB client, *smbclient*, allows you to access SMB servers from UNIX systems. It provides a user interface similar to the command-line-oriented FTP client on UNIX systems. The following command queries the server for which shares it provides:

```
# smbclient -L <servername>
```

smbclient then displays a list of shares and their types (i.e., disks, printers, etc.):

```
# ./smbclient -L paranoia
Server time is Sun Mar 23 19:33:54 1997
Timezone is UTC-0.0
Server=[PARANOIA] User=[] Workgroup=[PARANOIA_GROUP] Domain=[]
      Sharename      Type      Comment
      ---------      ----      -------
      IPC$           IPC       Remote IPC
      ADMIN$         Disk      Remote Admin
      C$             Disk      Default share
      D$             Disk      Default share
      E$             Disk      Default share
      Tools          Disk      Workgroup Programming Tools


This machine has a browse list:

      Server      Comment
      ------      -------
      PARANOIA
#
```

The example shows that, in addition to the default shares for administrative purposes (ending with a $), we have a share called "Tools." The content of the output of the command *smbclient -L* resembles that of the UNIX command *showmount*, which displays which directories or filesystems are exported via NFS.

Access a share with the following command (analogous to mounting an NFS filesystem):

```
# smbclient \\\\Computername\\Sharename
```

Why are there so many backslashes? By SMB convention, a share is accessible on the network under the name *\\hostname\sharename*. However, since the backslash is a metacharacter that the UNIX shell interprets, we must override its special meaning for the shell by adding another backslash.

SAMBA provides the basic tool for recognizing shares on an NT server and testing whether they can be accessed without a password. Now we need to write a Perl script that handles the invocation of *smbclient* and transforms its output to the

SATAN database record format. We do this with the following script, saved as
smb.satan in the directory *~satan/bin*:

```
#!/usr/local/bin/perl5.001
#
# Report filesystems that are shared via Netbios file services.
# Find filesystems that are mountable without a password.
#
# version 1, Mon Dec 18 03:15:11 1995, marvin
#

$running_under_satan = 1;
require 'config/satan.cf';
require 'config/paths.pl';
require 'perl/misc.pl';

# where smbclient resides
$SMBCLIENT="/home2/src/samba-1.9.14/source/smbclient";

$usage="Usage: $0 target";
$timeout = $short_timeout;

# ascertain that we have a target
($#ARGV == 0) || die $usage;

$target = $ARGV[0];

$service = &basename($0, ".satan");
$severity = "x";
$status = "a";
$service_output = "";

# force output flush
$| = 1;

open(SMB, "$SMBCLIENT -L $target |") || die "$0: cannot run smb";
while(<SMB>) {
    chop;
    # ignore everything but disks
    next unless /^\s+((\S+)(\s+\S+)*)\s+Disk\s+((\S+\s*)*)/;
    $files=$1;
    $desc=$4;

    $trusted = "";
    $trustee = "";
    $service_output = "SMB share";
    if ($desc eq "") {
        $desc="no comment available for this share";
    }
    $text = "shares $files via SMB ($desc)";

    # try to mount with null password
    open (SMNT, "$SMBCLIENT \\\\\\\\$target\\\\'$files' '' \\
     2>/dev/null << _EOTEXT
```

```
        pwd
        quit
        _EOTEXT |");
            while (<SMNT>) {
                chop;
                # if the above pwd command succeeds,  we will match the line below
                next unless /^smb: \\> Current directory .*/;
                $trusted = "ANY\@ANY";
                $trustee = "$files\@$target";
                $service_output = "SMB share";
                $text = "shares $files via SMB with everyone ($desc)";
            }

            &satan_print();
        }
```

Let us examine more closely the most important elements of this script. The first *open()* command executes the command *smbclient -L $target*:

```
    open(SMB, "$SMBCLIENT -L $target |") || die "$0: cannot run smb";
```

Here the variable *$SMBCLIENT* was set in advance to contain the complete path of the program *smbclient*. We pass the target of our scan, *$target*, as a command-line argument. The pipe symbol (|) at the end of the argument for the *open()* command allows us to use the output of *smbclient* as input for our script.

The following while loop reads the output line by line. All lines not containing the word "Disk" are ignored; in this script we are interested only in shares that allow mounting file regions. If a line contains the word "Disk," the text to the left of that word is the share name and to the right is a descriptive comment; the variables *$files* and *$desc* sort this correspondingly. The regular expression for this is somewhat more complex because both *$files* and *$desc* can also contain blanks.

Next we try to mount the share; analogously to the first *open()* command, we now invoke *smbclient* with the command to mount the share *$target**$files* with a null password.

```
    open (SMNT, "$SMBCLIENT \\\\\\\\$target\\\\'$files' '' 2>/dev/null << _EOTEXT
    pwd
    quit
    _EOTEXT |");
```

Because the backslash is a metacharacter not only for the shell but also for Perl, we need to override this special meaning in both; as a result, each backslash in the share name now becomes a series of four! To test whether the mount was successful, we display the current directory with *smbclient* with the command *pwd* and then terminate with *quit*. These commands are passed to *smbclient* with simple input redirection.

The subsequent while loop reads the output line by line. If the *pwd* command was successful, which the output of *smbclient* indicates, the detected vulnerability is recorded in variables. *satan_print()* then handles output in SATAN database record format. The variables *$target, $service, $status, $severity, $trustee, $trusted, $service_output*, and *$text* correspond to the fields in the SATAN database record format.

We are almost done! Naturally SATAN must still be informed that it must execute the script; we enter this in *~satan/config/satan.cf* to execute the script with each normal scan, as follows:

```
@normal = (
        @light,
        'finger.satan',
        'tcpscan.satan 70,80,ftp,telnet,smtp,nntp,uucp,6000',
        'udpscan.satan 53,177',
        'rusers.satan?',
        'boot.satan?',
        'yp-chk.satan?',
        'smb.satan',
        );
```

It might be more intelligent to execute the script only if the target is an SMB server; otherwise it would be a waste. Here we write a question mark after the entry *smb.satan* to indicate that the execution should be conditional, and in *~satan/rules/todo* we specify under what conditions the script should run:

```
# If host is SMB server, run smb.satan
$service eq "netbios-ssn"                $target "smb.satan"
```

netbios-ssn is the Session Service (TCP/IP Port 139) where we recognize an SMB server.

Last but not least, we want to produce an HTML page to display information on the detected vulnerability. This page must reside in the directory *~satan/html/tutorials/vulnerability* and receives the name *SMB_share.html*. (Remember that the name of the page is extracted from the content of the variable *$service_output*; if this variable is modified, the name of the page must be adapted.)

To generally indicate that a scanned target is an SMB server, regardless of whether vulnerabilities were detected, we enter the corresponding ports in *~satan/rules/services* in the section SERVERS:

```
$service eq "netbios-ssn"                SMB
$service eq "netbios-ns"                 Netbios Name
```

Thus, on evaluation of the results SATAN indicates whether a target provides shares or is a NetBIOS name server.

SATAN in Large Networks

SATAN requires a certain amount of time to scan a host or a whole subnetwork. How long SATAN runs depends primarily on two factors: the hosts in the network and other devices with network capability.

The slowest host to scan is a PC under MS-DOS or Windows. This is not due to the PC hardware, but simply because PCs normally do not provide their own network services or run their own server processes. SATAN detects that a device is on the network because the PC responds to a ping. Further probes produce no feedback, and SATAN frequently waits for a timeout. Additional scanning delays ensue from networked printer switches and similar devices that frequently have only a minimal TCP/IP implementation and do not even respond to IP packets that they do not understand.

For scanning a complete subnetwork, SATAN's execution time is dependent on the number of hosts: the more hosts in the subnetwork, the longer it takes.

Scanning a subnetwork (with at most 254 connected hosts) can take hours. If larger networks are to be scanned, interactive mode becomes absurd; this would require sitting in front of the monitor for days just to press a key every couple of hours. Therefore it makes sense to handle larger scans in batch mode. SATAN can be controlled from the command line, as described earlier. However, the evaluation and the display of results then demands an interactive session. SATAN automatically starts in batch mode if the command line contains a target (a host or a network) for scanning. In addition, SATAN supports the following options:

−a level
: Severity of scans (0=light, 1=normal, 2=heavy)

−A decrement
: Value by which scan severity is decremented if dependent hosts are scanned

−c list
: Change SATAN's internal variables; takes an argument list in the form "variable=value;variable2=value2;..."

−d name
: Store results in the database "name"

−i
: Ignore previous results and rescan all hosts, even if there are results from previous scans

−l proximity
: Maximum nesting depth of dependencies

−o list

Only hosts in this list are scanned

−O list

Hosts in this list are excluded from scanning

−s

Subnetworks are expanded

−S statusfile
Use the specified name for the status file

−u

SATAN is running on an *untrusted host*

−U

SATAN is running on a *trusted host*; i.e., the SATAN host appears in *.rhosts*, *hosts.equiv*, or other files on hosts to be scanned

−t level

Default value for the timeout: 0=short, 1=medium, 2=long; times specified in *~satan/config/satan.cf* are used

−v

Enable debug information

−V

Output the version number

−z

If the severity of an attack becomes negative, continue with severity "0"

−Z

Stop if the severity of an attack attains the value "0"

All options need not be specified unless you want to deviate from the values specified in *~satan/config/satan.cf* (see the section "SATAN's Configuration File (satan.cf)" earlier in this chapter). For normal operation it is advisable to store customized default values in the configuration file and only in exceptional cases to change them in the command line.

It is best to embed the SATAN invocation in a small shell script. To scan a complete Class B network (65,536 possible address combinations), this script could take the following form:

```
count=0
netw=129.103
while [ $count -lt 256 ]
do
    # start SATAN with corresponding network name
    satan -d net$netw.$count -S stat.$netw.$count -s -u $netw.$count.1
    # increment counter
```

```
        count=`expr $count + 1`
    done
```

This shell script scans all subnetworks of the network 129.103 and stores the results in databases that have the network address as part of their names, i.e., net129.103.0, net129.103.1, etc. Thus the scan can run automatically overnight or over a weekend, with evaluation of the results following later. Note again that for SATAN a subnetwork always has the network mask 255.255.255.0. Even if the network actually employs a different network mask, the scans must always be structured in this way.

For multiple Class B or Class A networks, the approach would be analogous, possibly with an additional loop. A complete scan of a Class A network takes an extremely long time. If multiple Class A networks are in use, scanning cannot be done casually, but requires careful time planning. In the Internet environment one would seldom scan a complete large network, but would normally scan only selected hosts. For internal security audits, on the other hand, scanning the complete address space might indeed be appropriate. Large organizations have a greater chance of finding deviants, i.e., workgroups that have established free IP addresses and thus work in isolation from the rest of the company. Without such a wide-ranging scan, these are impossible to find. Cases where an organization occupies multiple Class A networks can be found, naturally not on the Internet, but certainly in company-internal networks that work with unofficial IP addresses.

The file *~satan/statusfile* reflects what SATAN has done during a batch run. Each command executed by SATAN is recorded there.

6

Detecting and Repelling SATAN Attacks

When You Become SATAN's Target

Naturally SATAN can be used for more than just security audits. You could become the target of an attack with SATAN when a potential intruder attempts to employ SATAN to find vulnerabilities in your system. Naturally, you want to avoid this, and you need to find out from which host, organization, or individual the attack came so that you can initiate measures against the attacker. Scanning foreign hosts without preliminary approval can have only one purpose—preparing for an intrusion attempt. You can and should take all technically feasible measures, independently of subsequent legal steps against the attacker.

Detecting attacks and protecting against them could be conflicting goals. You can protect yourself so well against an attack that you do not even notice that you have been attacked. In this case your system is secure, but because you do not know that you have been the target of an attack, you might be handicapped in defending against future attacks with possibly advanced methods.

Inversely, you can leave your system somewhat less bulletproof than current security measures would allow. Although this allows you to detect attacks when they occur, you always run the risk that you overlooked some loophole.

In any case, you need to carefully consider which approach to take before you connect to public networks like the Internet. Chapter 7, *Beyond SATAN*, treats security concepts in depth. Here it is important that you can detect SATAN attacks while the scan is in progress. SATAN is not a stealth tool that can intrude secretly and without detection. SATAN leaves unmistakable traces.

Recognizing a SATAN Attack

Detecting a SATAN attack is quite simple. The most prominent characteristic of a SATAN security audit is its scanning of the ports with the tools *tcp_scan* and *udp_scan*. Each time that any system attempts to make a huge number of connections to incrementing port numbers on your system, you can be certain that a SATAN attack is underway. Depending on the probe level, SATAN's attempts to misuse individual services will be reflected in the log files of the respective services.

Various tools can help you to detect such attacks. They all monitor the subnetwork or system on which they run; on a certain preset number of connection attempts per minute, they trigger an alarm, sending mail to the administrator, ringing a pager, writing log messages, or sending an SNMP trap to a network management system. Although these tools were written for (or against?) SATAN, they help to detect other kinds of attacks as well: any tool that runs a security audit on a host must scan all TCP and UDP ports to determine which network services are running where, and therefore can be detected.

Gabriel

The archangel Gabriel—appropriately for a program that protects against SATAN—served as the namesake for this tool. Written by Los Altos Technologies Inc., it is available as freeware on the FTP server *ftp.lat.com*. Gabriel was written in C and shell scripts; thus it requires no Perl interpreter or similar tools. Binaries for SunOS 4 (Solaris 1) and Solaris 2 are included in the distribution.

For monitoring network traffic, Gabriel employs the system program *etherfind* (SunOS 4) or *snoop* (Solaris 2). These programs permit monitoring of all packets that reach their host on its network connection, which need not be all packets that are actually underway on the network. If the host has a high CPU load or the network connection is very busy, *etherfind* can lose some packets. This does not impair Gabriel's utility, for an individual packet is not so important. The purpose is to locate a host that is generating a large number of connection requests, and, given the number of connection attempts that SATAN produces, a single lost packet does not matter.

Gabriel launches these programs and stores their output, sorted by host, in a linked list. Periodically Gabriel checks the list for a host that makes connections to other hosts on the network conspicuously often. If Gabriel finds such a case, it sends a message via *syslog* to a server. On this server a shell script checks the log entries and thereupon initiates actions: an email to the system administrator, ringing a pager, etc. This separation of client and server makes Gabriel a useful tool in larger networks: It suffices to run a single client in each network segment; this client continuously checks the overall subnetwork, reads all network traffic, and analyzes it. The clients of all segments report to a central server whenever they detect an attack; from there the administrator is alerted.

Gabriel is also well-suited for continuous use for network control. The clients can be configured so that they transmit a "heartbeat" at regular intervals; this is a short message conveying that they are still active, even if there is no attack to report. By adapting the Gabriel server, you can easily achieve fully automated checking.

Installing Gabriel on Suns is simple; scripts are available for installing both the server and the client. Solaris 1 and Solaris 2 are recognized automatically and the appropriate client is installed. The scripts are interactive and prompt for the needed data (server name) and test whether *etherfind* or *snoop* is really available. You need to manually edit only the configuration file for the server, *gabriel.conf*:

```
warning     mail     /usr/ucb/mail -s "SATAN warning" marvin@infoac.rmi.de
alert       log      /var/adm/log/gabriel.alog
info        log      /var/adm/log/gabriel.ilog
```

This file specifies which actions are to be started at which *syslog* log levels. Heartbeats, etc. are stored under the level *info*; *alert* indicates normal SATAN attacks, while *warning* indicates a heavy scan. Naturally, this distinction between normal and heavy scans functions only if SATAN is running in the standard configuration and has not been adapted by its user. In the example, information messages and normal scans are logged, and only heavy scans invoke a message with the subject "SATAN warning" to the administrator.

The program *gabriel_tester* allows you to test whether the installation really works. This test program does the same as SATAN's *tcp_scan*: it attempts to make connections to many network services.

Although Gabriel runs splendidly on Suns, adapting it to other systems is not always easy. Programs such as *etherfind* and *snoop* are available for most operating systems. However, they bear different names for each UNIX variant, and neither their command-line arguments nor their output is standardized. Thus modifications in the source code are necessary in any case. Furthermore, Gabriel relies on a *syslog* service with network capability, which is not always the case with System V variants and which has some problems from a security viewpoint. *syslog* is a potential target for "denial of service" attacks, and an advanced attacker could thereby disable Gabriel by flooding the *syslog* daemon so that Gabriel's messages become lost in a deluge of log messages. Nevertheless, Gabriel is currently the best tool for detecting SATAN attacks.

Courtney

Courtney is a script developed by CIAC, the Computer Incident Advisory Capability of the U.S. Department of Energy. It can be downloaded from the WWW server of CIAC at the URL *http://ciac.llnl.gov/ciac/ToolsUnixNetMon.html.*

Courtney is a Perl script and requires Perl Version 5. To monitor local network traffic, it uses *tcpdump*, a widespread freeware port monitor that works similarly to *etherfind* or *snoop* on Solaris.

Courtney works almost identically to Gabriel. Courtney starts *tcpdump*, sorts its output in a list, and evaluates it. Depending on invocation parameters, on a detected attack a syslog entry is generated, a message is sent to the system administrator, or a message is simply written on the terminal.

Courtney lacks the feature of multiple clients reporting to a central server, so it can be used only for a single host or for a subnetwork. The typical application for Courtney is in smaller networks that are not further subdivided into segments.

The greatest hurdle to using Courtney is the compilation of *tcpdump*. Depending on your system, this can mean significant effort. On some architectures *tcpdump* is not particularly stable. If you need to monitor multiple subnetworks and you have Sun workstations, then using Gabriel is normally easier.

Routers

Workstations are not particularly well-suited for monitoring network traffic and analyzing the number of established connections. Dedicated hardware does the job better, faster, and usually more economically. Since network traffic passes routers or bridges on its way from the sender to the receiver, it makes sense to check there to see if a SATAN attack is in progress. The data needed for this check is present on the router anyway for accounting purposes, and a periodic check of a connection list demands little additional CPU time. The manufacturers of routers have long since realized this, and so such checks (as well as components of circuit-level firewalls) can increasingly be found in the firmware of routers.

If the task of detecting SATAN attacks is transferred to active network components in this way, you need to be aware that a router (or a bridge) sees only the traffic that passes through it. None of the traffic within a subnetwork can be checked with this solution. If you expect attacks from within your subnetwork, Gabriel or Courtney are your only options.

Repelling SATAN and Other Attacks

The above tools help you to detect a SATAN scan, but naturally detection alone does not suffice. You don't simply want to know that you are being attacked, you want to defend yourself!

The best protection against SATAN and similar tools is proper configuration of the host—which includes not only correct configuration of the services that you do need to run, but also not running services that you do not need. The fewer processes you have running, the less you have to worry about security issues that might crop up at a later date. If you have run SATAN yourself and corrected the vulnerabilities that were detected, then your host is already quite secure.

We distinguish the following two cases:

- Protecting one or more hosts, even against attacks from within your subnetwork

- Protecting an entire network for which the possibility of attacks from within the subnetwork can be neglected (trusted colleagues)

These cases are quite different. The former demands protective measures on individual hosts, so it must be possible to install the corresponding tools there. This means that you must have root privileges on the hosts that are to be protected. In addition, you must consider that there might be dependencies on the part of already installed products, which means that the security tools can impair the functioning of other software.

In the second case the individual hosts need not be considered further. The protective measures must be applied at the points of contact to other subnetworks, at the routers. The appropriate configuration of filtering routers or the utilization of firewalls can reduce network traffic between subnetworks to only what is absolutely necessary. Connections can be authenticated and logged, which also helps to realize effective protection.

tcp-wrapper and Similar Tools

The best protection against unauthorized use of a network service is to limit access to the service to a small group of PCs, workstations, or users. Unfortunately, standard UNIX does not provide this possibility, but assumes that the server programs themselves carry out authentication, either with password protection or by checking the name or the IP address of the client. However, even if the server does carry out such a check, the server has already been started! As an example, if a client wants to connect to an FTP server, *inetd* will start the FTP daemon as specified in its configuration file */etc/inetd.conf.* This daemon will then carry out the authentication by asking for a login and a password. However, if the authentication routines in the daemon already contain exploitable bugs, an intruder can take advantage of vulnerabilities on this server before the built-in authentication takes hold.

Therefore, we need to employ a protection program at the point where the individual servers are started. This is the only place to ensure that only authorized clients make contact with the server.

Fortunately, there is such a point in all modern UNIX variants: *inetd*, the central Internet daemon that monitors all available ports and launches the associated server when a connection is made. Here *inetd* reads the configuration file */etc/inetd.conf*, which specifies which programs are to be started on which ports. For example, the telnet daemon is started as follows:

```
telnet stream tcp nowait root /usr/sbin/in.telnetd in.telnetd
```

At the left is the name of the service, here *telnet*; *inetd* finds the corresponding port number in the file */etc/services*, which records all known services and their port numbers. After the specification of the transport protocol to be used (here TCP), the above line shows the user ID under which the server program is to be started (here */usr/sbin/in.telnetd* under user ID *root*). The subsequent fields are command-line arguments for the server; in any case the program name must be entered here again, even if no arguments are needed. (The entries in this file differ somewhat depending on the UNIX variant; instead of *in.telnetd*, the telnet daemon might be called *telnetd* or reside in a directory other than */usr/sbin*.)

Instead of the usual server program with a complete path, you can enter a protection program here that first checks whether a client is authorized to use the service and then, assuming authorization, starts the server. *tcp-wrapper* is a software package that implements access control for UNIX network services. Its name derives from its function: like a wrapper, it surrounds all TCP/IP-based services. An important component of *tcp-wrapper* is the program *tcpd*, which is entered in place of the normal server in the file *inetd.conf*:

```
telnet stream tcp nowait root /usr/local/wrap/tcpd in.telnetd
```

Analogously, set *tcpd* as the server for FTP, finger, and any other services. Recall that after you modify the file */etc/inetd.conf*, you must tell *inetd* to reload its configuration! This is normally done by sending the *inetd* process a hang-up signal (SIGHUP), for instance, with the command `kill -HUP`. Unfortunately there are small differences among the *inetd* daemons in various UNIX variants; you might find that an *inetd* does not accept modifications to already running services. In this case you must first comment out the service (place a # at the beginning of the line) and send a SIGHUP, then remove the comment character, enter *tcpd* as server, and again send a SIGHUP to force *inetd* to reload the configuration file.

Apart from *inetd.conf,* you need not change any system file for configuration. On the basis of the arguments (here *in.telnetd*), *tcpd* knows which service to start.

On making a connection, *tcpd* checks the files */etc/hosts.allow* and */etc/hosts.deny* to determine whether a client is authorized to access a service. These files specify rules for deciding whether to grant access. First the file */etc/hosts.allow* is consulted and access is granted if it contains a rule that matches the client. If this is not the case, *tcpd* checks in */etc/hosts.deny* for a rule that forbids access. If there is no restriction here, the client is granted access. Thus, the sequence of entries in these files is important. If a line is found in */etc/hosts.allow* that permits a host to use a certain service, then it does not help to have an entry in */etc/hosts.deny* that blocks access.

The rules have the following general form:

```
services : clients : optional commands
```

As an example, we take an */etc/hosts.allow* file:

```
finger,tftp : .dg5kx.de,194.194.194.0/255.255.255.0 : (/usr/ucb/mail -s
"access by %c" root)&
```

This file grants access to the services finger and TFTP to all clients in the domain *dg5kx.de* and to all hosts in network 194.194.194.0. When there is access to these services, an email message with a subject line containing the name or the IP address of the client is to be sent to *root.*

In combination with the file */etc/hosts.deny* containing only the following entry,

```
ALL : ALL
```

access to these two services would be reserved for hosts in the domain *dg5kx.de* or at network address 194.194.194.*.

By adapting this small example to your host, you can achieve a quite secure configuration. The complete configuration of *tcp-wrapper* that exploits all its features is complex due to its powerful and numerous options, especially for a server that provides numerous network services. The included utilities *tcpdchk* and *tcpd-match* help you to check the file */etc/inetd.conf* and the rule files for *tcp-wrapper* for errors.

tcp-wrapper is available via anonymous FTP from *ftp.win.tue.nl* in the directory */pub/security.*

There are quite a number of software packages, some freeware, some proprietary, that provide similar functionality, sometimes in combination with simple system security audits. Among the freeware packages, *tcp-wrapper* is certainly the most widespread of these tools and thus also the most thoroughly tested. For UNIX System V Release 4, the program IPACL (*ftp://ftp.eunet.co.at/pub/network/ipacl/ipacl.tar.gz*)

provides a good alternative; it implements an access control mechanism as a Streams module. This module is then automatically loaded with the SVR4 auto-push mechanism whenever the IP device is accessed.

Commercial packages are normally very system-specific; check with the manufacturer of your host about the availability of such a wrapper.

However, there are some cases where *tcp-wrapper* and all similarly structured programs do not afford complete security, where a server program can start without being noticed by the wrapper. This is the case with most UDP-based services. Because UDP is not connection-oriented, a UDP server can never determine whether the client still needs its services. To avoid quasi-starting a new server process for each packet, the UDP server normally waits some seconds after each activity before it retires. Services that exhibit this behavior are designated by the keyword *wait* in the file */etc/inetd.conf.* If a new request arrives via the network during this time—regardless from which client!—this client is served as well. However, *tcp-wrapper* can determine only the first client that triggers the launching of the UDP services. No other clients can be detected, and so there is no access control in this case.

Note that a program like *tcp-wrapper* can only authenticate a request on the basis of the sender's IP address, meaning that it trusts that the sender of an IP packet writes his own IP address into the IP packet header. If IP packets are forged (see the section on IP-spoofing in Chapter 7), they can pass any restrictions that have been set up.

tcpd also cannot deliver additional security for RPC services that are started via the portmapper, because they are assigned their port numbers dynamically. However, here a somewhat secure portmapper or *rpcbind* can help.

Secure rpcbind/portmapper

The standard portmapper* delivered with normal operating systems has no feature for access restriction. portmapper is actually only a directory service: in response to a request for an RPC service, it creates the connection to an RPC service by providing a port number under which this service can be accessed. The portmapper poses security problems because several RPC services do not conduct any reasonable authentication. Additionally, the portmapper for some operating systems can function as a sort of relay station: it forwards requests from clients to the respective services. As a result, these services can no longer tell which client really needs to be serviced because the requests now seem to come from the local system.

---

* Under System V the portmapper is called *rpcbind.*

If a host exhibits this behavior, then, aside from introducing a patch, in case the vendor provides one, the only salvation is to switch to a secure portmapper. Such a portmapper can be downloaded from *ftp.win.tue.nl* under */pub/security/ portmap_4.tar.Z.*

This portmapper replaces the similar program distributed with the operating system. It builds on the *tcp-wrapper* package to realize access control analogously to the TCP and UDP services described above. It has the following additional features:

- No forwarding of requests to NFS (*mountd* and *nfsd* daemons), NIS, or itself

- Forwarding of other requests via a nonprivileged port

In the files */etc/hosts.allow* and */etc/hosts.deny*, rules define which clients have access to the portmapper:

```
/etc/hosts.allow:
    portmap: 194.194.194.0/255.255.255.0
/etc/hosts.deny
    portmap: ALL: (/usr/local/wrap/safe_finger -l @%h | mail root) &
```

The procedure for System V systems is analogous; here the portmapper is replaced by *rpcbind*. Contrary to the rules for *tcp-wrapper*, these rules cannot contain hostnames because this can cause a deadlock during NIS requests. You always have to work with IP addresses.

The great advantage of this version of portmapper is its access control and its logging mechanisms when unauthorized clients access the portmapper. Even if this does not achieve complete protection of all RPC services when direct communication with the services is possible without the detour via portmapper, this secure portmapper does represent an excellent early warning system. This alone suffices to justify installation of the package.

Filtering Routers and Firewalls

The most secure way to protect against attacks is to block such packets from entering your network. Modern filtering routers can test network traffic according to almost any rules; on the basis of source or target address, port numbers (and thus the type of services, since each network service occupies its own port), direction of connection, etc., they decide whether to allow the traffic.

Which ports to block must be decided on an individual basis. Due to differing security requirements, different rules apply for in-house routers than for routers that make connections to a customer network or to a firewall system.

Ideally, on an in-house network the network structure roughly corresponds to the organizational structure; the users' PCs or workstations are connected to the same

IP subnetwork as the server with which they work. In this case, *access lists* in the routers can greatly restrict access to these systems from the outside. Normally it should suffice to channel only email (SMTP), telnet or rlogin, FTP, and DNS through the router; for more stringent security requirements, telnet and FTP can be blocked. If other connections through a router are necessary, these can be restricted to individual hosts or subnetworks. For a CISCO router, an access restriction could take the following form:

```
access-list 106 permit tcp 0.0.0.0 255.255.255.255 194.194.194.0 0.0.0.255 eq 20
access-list 106 permit tcp 0.0.0.0 255.255.255.255 194.194.194.0 0.0.0.255 eq 21
access-list 106 permit tcp 0.0.0.0 255.255.255.255 194.194.194.0 0.0.0.255 eq 25
access-list 106 permit ip 0.0.0.0 255.255.255.255 194.194.194.2 0.0.0.255 eq 53
access-list 106 deny ip 0.0.0.0 255.255.255.255 0.0.0.0 255.255.255.255
```

The example is an *incoming access list*, restricting incoming traffic on an interface of the router. On the entire network 194.194.194.0, the ports for FTP (port 20 and 21), SMTP (port 25) and DNS (port 53) are accessible to everyone. All other traffic is blocked by the *deny* rule at the end.

The most secure approach is to block all connections by default and allow only the specified connections. This approach should be taken in any case for connections to outside networks. However, an Internet connection should never run via a filtering router alone; the use of a firewall system is urgently recommended.

Host routes are frequently entered in the routers instead of access lists to restrict access. At a glance this method seems to work; here, too, the specified clients can no longer pass the router. However, this method is relatively insecure because it can be circumvented by manipulations of the routing protocol. Likewise, filtering to restrict access to port numbers, etc. is not possible with host routes. An access list is preferable in any case, especially because routers can report violations against this access lists via *syslog*. A CISCO router can be configured for logging as follows:

```
access-list 106 deny tcp 0.0.0.0 255.255.255.255 0.0.0.0 255.255.255.255 eq 23
log
```

This access list blocks all telnet traffic (port 23) between any hosts. Violations of this rule are logged. Note, however, that it does not always make sense to log every violation of a rule, because the volume of logging data would soon become a deluge. For selected ports, on the other hand, logging—assuming an administrator evaluates the logs—can prove to be a fine early warning system that indicates when attacks are launched.

Note that a simple access list like the one above can authenticate only on the basis of the sender's IP address, meaning that it is possible to bypass it using forged IP packets. A more complex access list would also take into account which router interface a packet came in from, and throw away packets that have a source IP address belonging to an IP network that is local to another interface on the same router. See the section on IP spoofing in Chapter 7.

Significantly more secure than a filtering router is a firewall system. Routers recognize authorized clients only on the basis of addresses. For multiuser systems this can be a problem if all users of a system are not granted access. A firewall, on the other hand, enables authentication of individual users. Users are recognized via a password, a chip card, or both. The users can then be granted connections to selected services on selected hosts. References to firewalls appear in the appendix.

7

Beyond SATAN

Security Is More Than SATAN

So you have run SATAN, analyzed its output, and corrected the vulnerabilities that SATAN detected. Are your hosts secure now? No.

More precisely, you are secure with respect to SATAN attacks, but this does not imply comprehensive security. SATAN finds only a limited number of problems, and there are many more possibilities for breaking into a host via a network or for disturbing its normal operation than SATAN can find. This does not mean that SATAN contains errors or was poorly written. For purely technical reasons, SATAN simply cannot find some vulnerabilities because as an application program it is at the mercy of the underlying operating system and particularly the network software. A program at the application level can neither detect attacks aimed at this underlying level, nor detect attacks exploiting vulnerabilities in the transport protocol, nor provide protection against such attacks. (At least a *portable* application program cannot. It is, of course, possible to write an application that reads raw packets from the wire and that builds its own IP packets from scratch to scan for vulnerabilities. However, such a program would be highly system-dependent.)

Security encompasses more than just stuffing security holes at random. Naturally, this approach is not bad, for every vulnerability that we can eliminate is good. However, the administrator of a system is never blessed with the feeling of having found all vulnerabilities. There must be a methodology, a concept, for approaching the goal of maximum protection. Such a concept should not only make hosts on the network secure, but also should efficiently handle intrusions if they occur anyway. The second part of this chapter details such a security concept, identifies technical points to observe, and suggests organizational measures to be taken. Frequently the organizational changes are more extensive and work-intensive than the technical defensive measures.

What SATAN Does Not Find

It is important to understand that SATAN is a useful utility for finding several frequently occurring vulnerabilities in systems, but it is no panacea. Naturally, SATAN can find only problems that it recognizes and for which it has corresponding scripts. Security is a dynamic matter; new vulnerabilities are constantly emerging. Without extensions, SATAN cannot detect these.

Likewise, SATAN can detect only vulnerabilities that are due to erroneous configuration or software errors. SATAN cannot detect vulnerabilities that can be exploited only by a user who is already logged in normally on a host. Without any claim of completeness, the following sections enumerate several vulnerabilities of which a system or network administrator should be aware.

Eavesdropping

Network traffic can be monitored and tapped. Especially with bus networks like Ethernet, this is a reality that we simply have to live with. Any traffic on a LAN segment can be read by other stations on the same segment. This does not even require any special equipment like a LAN analyzer. Programs with this capability are either distributed with the operating system, such as *etherfind* and *snoop* for UNIX systems, or available as shareware or freeware, such as *ethload* for MS-DOS and *tcpdump* for UNIX.

This means that any data transferred as plain text can be read by others relatively easily. What is particularly alarming is that passwords are normally transferred as plain text. For telnet, *rlogin*, and FTP an eavesdropper can achieve easy access to a system by monitoring the LAN traffic and filtering out the passwords from the TCP/IP packets.

One-time passwords, i.e., passwords that are valid only for one login and that are invalidated immediately after use, are a good choice for better security. Even if an attacker manages to get your password by "sniffing" on the wire, it will be of no use to him since it is worthless after use. A number of products exist that implement one-time schemes; however, this is not standard for today's operating systems.

Encrypting all transferred data, both content and passwords, is the best protection against surveillance. If applications support encryption for data transfer, make use of this feature, especially if you are transferring sensitive information such as private data. Unfortunately the standard services like *rlogin* and telnet do not support encryption. For these services, there is the secure shell program *ssh* (see additional information at the URL *http://www.cs.hut.fi/ssh*). *ssh* replaces the standard *rlogin*, *rcp*, etc. clients and servers distributed with the UNIX operating system and features secure authentication of server and client in addition to encryption of passwords. However, using *ssh* requires that all clients working on a secure server support the *ssh* protocol. This is not a problem if all the hosts are UNIX workstations and have a C compiler to allow compiling *ssh*. On heterogeneous networks this can prove more problematic.

When using encryption, you should also think about the legal setting. Using cryptographic methods in a LAN is legally uncomplicated in some countries. However, in other countries encryption is forbidden (e.g., China) or permitted only with restrictions (e.g., France). For WAN connections, you first need to check whether the use of cryptographic software is permitted; the penalties for violations are sometimes draconian.

If encryption, for whatever reason, is not possible, then your only option is to restrict the hosts between which especially sensitive data transfers occur to their own network segments. In this way you can assure that users in other segments, decoupled by routers or bridges, cannot monitor the network traffic. It is a good idea to isolate the personnel department, finance, and bookkeeping, as well as the computing center and the system administration and operation in this way in their own subnetworks. This assures that private data and root passwords (for the computing center) do not fall into the wrong hands.

Spoofing

Spoofing usually designates attacks that in some way forge or falsify IP packets to obtain access to a host. The most frequent form is IP spoofing, sending IP packets with a forged return address. This even functions with routers, which normally check only the target address. A router cares only where a packet is going, not where it came from.

A dialog connection cannot be made in this way, at least not through a router. Because the attacked system cannot send the reply to this packet back to the attacker due to the forged address, the response goes to the real owner of the address instead (this is standard IP routing). Figure 7-1 shows such a scenario schematically.

But even without a dialog it is possible to intrude into a system, e.g., with a file transfer. In a "usual" attack pattern, someone would forge the address of a host listed in an *.rhosts* file in order to copy another *.rhosts* file there using *rsh*. The file the attacker sends will then contain the correct name of the attacking host, i.c., the name matching its real, non-spoofed address, thus enabling interactive access. Because the attacker can exactly predict, on the basis of the specification of TCP/IP and the application protocol, which TCP packets need to be sent when, this

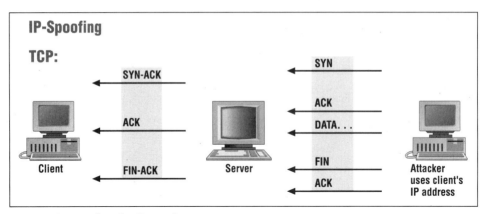

Figure 7-1. Data flow for IP spoofing

allows writing a tool to automate these attacks. Such attacks do take place on the Internet.

In Figure 7-1 a client (right) with a forged address makes a TCP/IP connection to a server. It sends a SYN (synchronize: a request for a connection) to the server. The server confirms the connection request with a SYN-ACK (synchronize acknowledge). However, the ACK is sent to the real owner of the IP address and so does not reach the attacker. Since the attacker can predict which packets need to be sent when, this is no problem; the attacker simply assumes the ACK and sends its data packets. The subsequent termination of the connection occurs in the same way: the attacker sends a FIN (request to terminate a connection) and can then terminate the connection.

The real client and rightful owner of the address can react in two ways to the ACKs that it receives. With a standard TCP implementation, it responds to packets that it cannot understand with a RST (reset) to indicate that an error has occurred. This normally induces the server to break the connection. To circumvent this, the attacker first disables the real client he is impersonating with a *SYN storm;* i.e., he bombards the client with requests for connection and so, overloading it for a short time, delays or prevents the termination of the connection.

Unfortunately, since RFC 1644 there has been another method for circumventing the server breaking the connection: an attacker can simply combine the connection request, data transfer, and connection termination in one TCP packet that contains both the SYN and FIN flags and data. In this way, data transfer has occurred before the actual owner of the address can react. In practice, some minimal TCP/IP implementations simply (although illegally) ignore packets that they do not understand—which makes things easy for the attacker.

Falsifying UDP/IP packets is particularly easy. Because UDP is a connectionless protocol, on receipt of data there is no means within the IP protocol to determine whether the sender's identity is authentic. Here only the application protocol itself can test the authenticity of the sender.

Fortunately, you can relatively easily protect against IP spoofing attacks. A filtering router suffices by using an access list to filter out all packets that come from an outside network but use a source address in the local network. Nevertheless, this cannot protect against attacks from within the local network, which do not pass a router.

There is another way of IP spoofing, which makes it possible to circumvent the above-mentioned restriction of passing routers and getting packets back to the attacker. This method would enable an attacker to open a dialog connection using a spoofed address. This uses IP source routing. With source routing, you can specify the way a packet should go when traversing a network, regardless of what the default IP routes configured in a router say. When a computer receives an IP packet with the source route option set, it will honor this option and send the response packets back the same way the requests came in, even if the routing tables say otherwise.

Your best defense against this is to not allow source routing at all in routers. Source routing was introduced years ago as a way of sending packets along known and trusted paths on the Internet. It is, however, used only rarely now, and is not necessary for normal network operation, and you will not lose any connectivity by simply switching it off. Issuing a command like

```
no ip source routing
```

should be one of your first actions when configuring a router.

Many application protocols can also be spoofed. Routing protocols, such as the widespread RIP, the Routing Information Protocol, serve as an example. RIP distributes information about the path that an IP packet must take in the network from the sender to the receiver. The router, whether a dedicated router or a UNIX or other system configured as a router, sends the routing information as a UDP broadcast, and all systems that receive such a broadcast adapt their routing tables in their kernels correspondingly. Since RIP carries out no authentication of whether the sender of such a broadcast is authorized to distribute routing information, but indiscriminately believes whatever is distributed on the network, the door is open to abuse. An intruder could employ falsified RIP packets to direct network traffic along new routes (e.g., for surveillance purposes) or at least to noticeably disrupt operation.

Here, too, access lists afford protection by accepting and forwarding routing information only from selected systems. In combination with IP spoofing, however, even access lists for RIP can be deceived. Therefore it makes sense to use, at least in a backbone, other routing protocols that, even if they do not always use better authentication procedures, are at least harder to falsify due to their complex structure.

In practice, in the backbone area, protocols such as OSPF or the proprietary protocol EIGRP are often used, and these are then translated to RIP outside the backbone. This allows you to profit in the backbone from the significantly better functionality of modern routing protocols while you can still use dynamic routing for peripheral devices, which often support no protocol other than RIP. This way the router refuses to accept any updates of its routing tables via the RIP protocol.

ICMP

ICMP, the Internet Control Message Protocol, is employed to report error states to the hosts in an IP network. This does not mean transfer errors in the normal sense, but errors in routing, overloads in lines or network connections, etc. ICMP employs IP to transfer messages, but is itself not a transport protocol such as TCP and UDP. However, ICMP can be seen as part of IP (every standard IP implementation also supports ICMP).

Thus an attacker can use falsified ICMP packets to create artificial error situations, and so detour data traffic to other routes. Other possibilities range from disturbing data flow all the way to completely breaking a connection.

The ICMP echo command used to test the existence of a connection between two hosts is the *ping* command. ICMP also has other commands that can be abused by an attacker to disrupt network traffic, including the following:

Destination unreachable
> This indicates that an individual host or an entire network cannot be reached, e.g., due to a routing problem. An attacker can force termination of a connection by sending such a falsified packet.

TTL exceeded
> This packet indicates that an IP packet has passed too many routers and thus raises suspicion that it has landed in an endless loop among hosts. Falsified packets of this nature can also disrupt data flow.

Source quench
> A *source quench* is sent when a host receives too much data too fast and wants to brake the sender. An attacker can exploit this to bring a host on the network almost to a standstill.

Redirect

> Redirect packets are sent by routers when, for route optimization reasons, a host should use another router on the same network. A host that receives such a packet will change its routing table in its kernel for the network or the individual host. Thus an attacker can redirect network traffic to new routes or bring it to its knees if a host is redirected to a nonexistent router.

The simplest protective measure against ICMP attacks is filtering out ICMP with a filtering router or firewall. When completely denying ICMP traffic from entering your network, the ensuing loss of functionality is often nearly negligible. It might confuse users on the local network that the *ping* command no longer works via the router, but the applications still run. This simply requires some explanation that *ping* is no longer a reliable test for the reachability of a host or network.

However, you might encounter spurious problems with packets that have the IP "Don't Fragment" (DF) bit set and that exceed the maximum length for a packet on an intermediate router. The safe way is to just filter out the above ICMP messages; and let other ICMP packets pass. Most modern firewalls will let you select which ICMP packets to drop and which to pass on.

Authentication and DNS

Classical UNIX authentication is host-based, that is, it tests the name of a client to see if it is authorized to use a service. This is the case for the usual *r*-services (*rlogin*, *rcp*, *rsh*, etc.) as well as for X Windows and many application programs. Naturally, user-oriented authentication would be better, because the host-based test does not distinguish different users on a multiuser system; however, it does provide a certain level of security.

Although this authentication approach does function, it is somewhat deceptive because it relies on unambiguous and certain assignment of a network address to a name. However, the reliability of that assignment is far less self-evident than we would like to believe.

If you use an */etc/hosts* file to resolve names to addresses and vice versa, then you have everything under your control and there is no security risk. Utilizing DNS changes the picture; here control is passed to someone else and trust is placed in an external DNS server. Anyone who operates a DNS server on the Internet could assign an IP address to an arbitrary host and domain name, as explained below.

When a client submits a request to a server, the server attempts to establish the client's name on the basis of the IP address. Let us consider an example where the client has the address *194.193.192.1* and the name *attacker.badguys.org* and the server is named *morla.rmi.de*. The server will query DNS for the name of *1.192.193.194.in-addr.arpa*, where *in-addr.arpa* is the pseudo-domain in which

DNS administers the assignment of address to name. If the attacker operates a DNS server, this enables the following entry in the name server files for *reverse mapping* for the network *194.193.192.0*:

```
1         PTR         morla.rmi.de.
```

Thereby the attacker is masquerading as a host in the domain of the target server, and even, as in the example, assumes the identity of the target itself although the correct entry would be the following:

```
1         PTR         attacker.badguys.org.
```

In this way the attacker can attempt to circumvent authentication with *.rhosts* or */etc/hosts.equiv* files. If you use a Java-capable WWW browser, this can mean that arbitrary Java programs can be executed on your Java client, although you might have the illusion of security.

Protect yourself against such attacks by having applications that rely on the client name for authentication always make double queries to DNS, by first resolving the address of the client to a name and then reversing the query for which the IP address corresponds to the name. If the double query produces a contradiction, i.e., if the IP address from the second query does not match the original one, there is a high probability of a falsified DNS entry, and the request must be ignored. However, this can only be done by the programmer that writes the application. The user should be aware that everything in DNS does not necessarily reflect the truth.

CGI scripts

Due to the widespread dissemination of WWW servers on the Internet and increasingly on intranets (company-internal networks) as well, a new category of security problems has emerged. Web servers employ CGI scripts to execute programs that produce dynamic Web pages. Such scripts are used in all WWW applications that do more than display a simple, static page. Each Web server that provides chat space, enables database research, or supplies HTML forms employs a CGI script.

CGI, the Common Gateway Interface, is the specification for passing parameters to the executing script. While a form normally specifies which parameters are passed to a script, nothing prevents a user from trying to invoke a CGI script with other invocation parameters. Unfortunately, many of the usual scripts have been kept quite simple and test the validity of neither the passed parameters themselves nor their contents. Thus through a suitable choice of parameters, an attacker can persuade a poorly written CGI script to execute almost any shell command under the Web server's user ID.

This kind of vulnerability is particularly critical because TCP wrappers, filtering routers, firewalls, etc. provide no protection. The execution of these scripts is intended; the author wants to provide users with the script's service. However, a router, TCP wrapper, etc. cannot test the parameters.

For protection against the abuse of CGI scripts, you should observe the following points:

- Web servers should never run under the user ID *root*. A nonprivileged user ID, such as *www*, suffices to operate the server. If something does go wrong, this at least assures damage control by preventing an intruder from executing commands as superuser. Every Web server can be configured so that, after starting and binding on WWW standard port 80, it assumes a different user ID.

- You must make sure that only the CGI scripts that are really needed reside in the directory *~/cgi-bin/*. Corpses left over from tests or old versions of scripts must be deleted.

- All CGI scripts must be programmed so that even with erroneous parameters they do not deliver surprising results; they must thoroughly test all parameters and be robust against erroneous input. In particular, assure that line feeds, special characters, and shell metacharacters that might appear in parameters do not cause undesired behavior.

- Avoid shell scripts as CGI scripts; they are too easy to abuse.

You will find a lot more to think about in the WWW security FAQ, located at *http://www.genome.wi.mit.edu/WWW/faqs*. This is a must-read if you are running your own WWW server. It covers both general topics like the secure setup of web servers and CGI scripts and server-specific topics.

The Security Policy

It is important to consider more than just the technical dimension of computer security, so that you can detect as many vulnerabilities as possible and take countermeasures.

There will always be vulnerabilities that are not familiar to you. Security is a dynamic matter. New vulnerabilities are constantly being found; new programs constantly appear on the market that pose new problems and new quirks. Satisfactory security can be achieved only if your measures cover these possibilities as well. Although no program can be written to protect against yet unknown threats, you can have a finished plan for how to detect attempted intrusions and what to do when you discover an attack or even an intrusion.

The objective of such a plan is to react immediately. Normally the first reaction to an intrusion is panic; no one seems to know what to do and whom to inform. In particular, if the press learns that there has been an intrusion at a company, it is important that someone competent be ready immediately with information rather than letting insecurity reign, as we so often see.

The creation of a security policy encompasses the following phases, which are discussed in the subsequent sections:

1. Status-quo analysis
2. Requirements analysis
3. Threat analysis
4. Policy creation
5. Policy implementation
6. Training
7. Validation
8. Update

Status-Quo Analysis

The status-quo analysis phase serves to determine the initial status: Where are we now? Which measures are already implemented? In practice this analysis is often astoundingly difficult because it requires first determining which network services are used at all and which communication relationships exist internally and to external companies and organizations. This is difficult because many procedures and communication paths sprouted over time, and there is often no longer anyone knowledgeable who can provide information about them.

A status-quo analysis often approaches a puzzle in which all parts and information first have to be collected and assembled before a clear picture emerges. However, it is absolutely necessary to complete this task before taking any technical measures for security; otherwise, only subaspects are considered and no comprehensive security can be achieved.

Requirements Analysis

What are the actual security requirements? Clearly you want a maximum, but which data and which hosts are really worth protecting and how much time or money is it worth?

Answering these questions is the task of the requirements analysis phase. Here you need to determine which files or data transfers need to be protected from whom. The insights gained here also help you to concentrate data worth protecting on as few hosts and subnetworks as possible. For the actual security policy, this also facilitates the task of putting technical measures in place.

Deliberating what damage could occur if data was destroyed or sensitive data became public helps to assess how much time and money to invest in security. Indeed, it does not make sense to invest more money in defensive measures than the data is worth. The assessment of potential damage is not always easy because the consequences of an intrusion can seldom be expressed in monetary form. Aside from direct costs, damage can occur from the following:

- Image damage when an intrusion becomes public and customers or partners lose confidence in your computing center or company

- Lost time and production until the encroached host or network runs perfectly again and all data is restored

- Indirect costs due to lost business if research results, customer data, etc. fall into the wrong hands

- Legal consequences, e.g., due to the revelation of private data through an intrusion

Decisions must be made on an individual basis to determine which of these points apply.

Threat Analysis

This military-sounding term addresses this simple question: from whom do we need to be protected, and from which sources might a potential intrusion come?

Fundamentally, during the threat analysis phase, we must distinguish between problems from outside the local network and intrusion attempts from within. The two differ in terms of both the kinds of protective measures to be taken—technical and organizational—and how these measures are carried out.

According to statistics, by far the most sabotage attempts come from within. However, we can assume that these are usually problems of system security (such as badly defined access privileges) or cases from nontechnical areas (such as embezzlement). The Internet, on the other hand, tends to be a source of technically refined intrusion attempts. Here we must distinguish between serious intrusion attempts and rather playful attempts; if you sound the big-time alarm each time the firewall reports a failed login attempt as *login guest, password guest*, you might be dealing with an alarm every couple of hours.

Policy Creation

From the data acquired from the status-quo analysis, the requirements analysis, and the threat analysis phases, during the policy creation phase we can derive which measures need to be taken to achieve reasonable protection. What is to be done specifically depends so greatly on the individual case that it is difficult to give general advice. In any case, the following points need to be considered:

- How can an intrusion be detected?

- Which tools are practical for securing hosts and what possibilities are available for protecting the entire network?

- What is your objective when an attempted intrusion occurs—do you want to catch the intruder, or do you want to capsule off the network to control damage?

- What kind of organization must be created to effectively handle the technical resources and to enable rapid reaction?

Often the technical questions are easiest to answer. After the constraints established in the requirements analysis, and considering the available hardware platform, often only a few programs, firewall solutions, etc. remain as candidates for implementation.

More difficult and more time-consuming are the organizational questions. All security programs, wrappers, and firewalls combined are useless if no one is on site to evaluate the log files and to make competent decisions. It is absolutely necessary that someone can always be reached who, in case of an emergency, can not only deliver the technical support, but who also has the necessary decision-making authority and freedom to determine what must be done. In an emergency, the situation must never arise in which the administrator on site must first wait until the boss arrives to decide what to do next.

A key question is: what is the primary objective in the event that a serious attack or even a successful intrusion is detected? Do you try to catch the intruder, or do you pull the plug and take your system off the network to minimize damage? In the former case you bear the risk that damage can increase while you are searching for the host and login from which the attack comes. In the latter case you have mastered the situation on a short-range basis, but you will likely become the target of an attack again soon. While the attacker might not complete the intrusion, repeated attacks will certainly manage to hinder the work of legitimate users of the system.

Normally, the objective of your attack reaction policy should be to trace and catch the attacker. In any case, it is important to decide in advance which course to follow, to make it part of your policy, and to adhere to this course in the event that an attack does occur. As a rule, damage increases if you do not adhere to your policy.

Policy Implementation

Naturally, the policy created during the previous phase needs to be implemented; it must not simply be put on a shelf to collect dust. Normally, all points of the security policy would not be implemented at once, so it makes sense to set up a schedule for the introduction of technical and organizational measures.

The planned implementation must be documented painstakingly so that a plan is available later that reflects what has been installed and how it works. Ideally, during the implementation phase a checklist should evolve that allows even an inexperienced administrator to find out what is running where and how it is to be used.

Training

On-site training of the administrators or operators is necessary so that they can handle the software and understand the security policy. Indeed, the purpose of a security policy is not merely to reach a secure state once, but to consistently ensure security over time. However, this requires assuring that new programs, hosts, and networks are planned and administered just as securely as the existing infrastructure. This can be achieved on a long-range basis only if the administrators live and breathe the security policy.

Training for users is just as important. Users often have a rather naive view of security and do not really want to believe that some services offered by a computer or a network can be insecure. This is understandable from the users' viewpoint! Their goal is to use the host for their work—their interest is not the internal workings of some transport protocol or daemon.

Thus, users must be sensitized to the subject of security and recognize that reasonable security measures are also in the interest of their work. This includes not just the network problems discussed in this book but also the areas of system security: secure passwords that password cracking programs like *crack* cannot guess, secure permissions, etc. Likewise, the frequently expressed fear that security measures impose unacceptable hindrances on daily work can be countered only with information and training. It must be made clear that security is in fact a gain, that the greater confidence in computers and applications alike that is achieved by good security saves more time in the long run than is lost by having to properly authenticate before starting a session.

In particular, each user must know whom to contact when a security problem is suspected.

Validation and Update

As we have said, security is a dynamic matter. After implementation of the security policy, there is no time for kicking back and relaxing because security has been achieved. Only regular testing of the network and all connected hosts can provide long-range security. Even a network itself is not a static matter, but changes and grows over time.

The following steps should be carried out at regular intervals:

- Audit your systems. For example, regularly test all user passwords with *crack* or similar programs.

- Audit your networks, using SATAN or another security scanner of your choice.

- Continue to update the security-related documentation—antiquated, erroneous information can be worse than none.

- Adapt the security policy to new requirements.

It is often a good idea to refrain from carrying out the security audits and validation yourself, and instead to pass this to another department or contract it to another company. The reason is that, over time, a certain internal blindness sets in. In a security policy designed internally, other people can find errors more readily than you can because they approach the matter from a different perspective.

Further Reading

This book has opened discussions on several aspects of network security: vulnerabilities in network services and how to correct them, protocol-related vulnerabilities, insecurity due to scripts executed by network daemons, etc. And design of a security policy, the only possible foundation for really comprehensive security, was discussed.

Exploring these subjects in greater depth is beyond the scope of this book. However, if you want to delve deeper into computer security, beyond the possibilities afforded by SATAN, then the following references to standards and publications should help you get started. This is not intended to be a comprehensive bibliography. Instead, this appendix presents a (necessarily biased to my own tastes) must-read list for every system and network administrator.

Publications

Generally recommended reading on the subject of security policies is the *Site Security Handbook*:

J. Paul Holbrook and Joyce K. Johnson, Ed., *Site Security Handbook*. RFC 1244, FYI 8.

There you will find instructions for designing your security concept and for handling attacks before, during, and after an intrusion. The handbook also includes a comprehensive list of further reading.

This RFC (Request For Comment) and all others can be downloaded via anonymous FTP from the server *ftp.isi.edu* in the directory */in-notes*, and from many other FTP servers.

Instructions for improving the security of UNIX systems appear in the following publication:

David A. Curry, "Improving the Security Of Your UNIX System," SRI International, 1990.

This publication is available from *http://www.telstra.com.au/pub/docs/security/ sert-doc/curry.ps.Z.*

This paper contains many instructions for secure configuration and passwords, as well as tips on detecting intrusions and establishing reasonable monitoring of your system. A checklist for auditing your computer and an extensive list of additional material complement the paper. Although the publication is some years old, it is well worth reading because the vulnerabilities discussed there are still problems today.

Dan Farmer and Wietse Venema posted a scenario on Usenet on December 2, 1993:

Dan Farmer and Wietse Venema, "Improving the Security of Your Site by Breaking Into it," 1993.

This paper can be downloaded from *ftp.win.tue.nl/pub/security/admin-guide-to-cracking.101.Z.* In a humorous way, the paper describes how an intrusion via the Internet could take place by exploiting frequently occurring configuration errors in network software. The content of the paper is closely related to SATAN, and an HTML version of it is part of SATAN's documentation.

If you plan to install a firewall, you cannot do without the following two books:

William R. Cheswick and Steven M. Bellovin. *Firewalls and Internet Security.* Addison-Wesley, 1994.

D. Brent Chapman and Elizabeth D. Zwicky. *Building Internet Firewalls.* O'Reilly & Associates, 1995.

These two books—also known as the Old Testament and the New Testament on Firewalls—comprehensively describe the kinds of firewalls, how they function, which threats a firewall guards against, and which dangers firewalls cannot handle. In addition, the books contain countless instructions for system and network security as well as for the design of your own company-wide security concept. In particular, the List of Bombs in *Firewalls and Internet Security* shows some common vulnerabilities, some of which we have also covered in this book.

Last but definitely not least,

Simson Garfinkel and Gene Spafford, *Practical UNIX & Internet Security.* O'Reilly & Associates, 1996.

is a must-read for every system and network administrator. It extensively covers system and network security and has many examples that can be used to build your own set of tools to help in secure system administration.

Online Resources

Numerous mailing lists cover almost all aspects of computer security, from general discussions of concepts to highly specialized subjects involving security problems on specific architectures. At *http://www.iss.net/sec_info/maillist.html* you will find a good compilation of better-known mailing lists; this list is particularly helpful because it gives not only the less descriptive names of the mailing lists but also a short description of the topic of each list.

If you are involved with security, especially in the Internet environment, you can't afford not to subscribe to the mailing lists of the CERTs to obtain late-breaking reports of insecurities in network software and instructions for remedial measures. At *http://www.cert.org/* you will find instructions about which mailing lists the various CERTs maintain.

The bugtraq mailing list is a must for everybody interested in UNIX security. It is a full-disclosure mailing list for UNIX security holes: what they are, how to exploit them, and what to do to fix them. It is highly technical in nature, and you will benefit most from it if you have a good working knowledge of UNIX and IP networking. To subscribe, send mail to *listserv@netspace.org* with the words "subscribe bugtraq" in the body.

ntbugtraq is a similar mailing list, but devoted to Windows NT security. Similar to bugtraq, a good knowledge of Windows NT administration and networking will help you get the most out of it. To subscribe, send mail to *listserv@ntadvice.com* with the words "subscribe ntbugtraq firstname lastname" in the body (where firstname and lastname are your own first name and last name).

The firewalls mailing list proves interesting for anyone interested in information about security aspects of firewalls in general and the characteristics and peculiarities of the various firewall products in particular, or for those who want to join in the discussion. To subscribe to this list, send an email with the content (not the subject line!) "subscribe firewalls" to the address *majordomo@greatcircle.com*.

In Network News (Usenet) you will also find many groups that discuss security subjects. Table A-1 lists international newsgroups.

Table A-1. International Security Newsgroups

Newsgroup	Subject
alt.security	Security issues on computer systems (not moderated)
alt.security.index	References to interesting postings in alt.security (moderated)
comp.os.netware.security	Netware security issues
comp.security.announce	Announcements from the CERT about security (moderated)
comp.security.firewalls	Anything pertaining to network firewall security
comp.security.misc	Security issues of computers and networks
comp.security.unix	Discussion of UNIX security
comp.virus	Computer viruses and security (moderated)
comp.lang.java.security	Security issues raised by Java
comp.security.pgp.*	Groups for discussions of PGP (Pretty Good Privacy)
comp.risks	Risks to the public from computers and users (moderated)

Likewise, the WWW contains many pages on network security. Information on SATAN is located at *http://wzv.win.tue.nl/* and *http://www.fish.com/satan.*

The web site *http://www.cs.purdue.edu/coast/coast.html* provides general information and numerous links to other pages. COAST (Computer Operations, Audit, and Security Technology) is an organization of the computer science faculty at Purdue University. This excellent web page provides numerous documents, tools, and links to other servers in all areas of security, from the most extensive archives to system and network security and on to viruses. Likewise, the web server of the CERTs at *http://www.cert.org/* provides valuable service. This site contains wide-ranging information and tools; it also allows you to subscribe to the CERTs' mailing lists.

For WWW security, the WWW security FAQ at *http://www.genome.wi.mit.edu/WWW/faqs* is highly recommended.

A good page for *exploits* (tools that detect and exploit vulnerabilities in UNIX systems), as well as many documents on network security, can be found at *http://www.deter.com/unix.*

These URLs can be used as launch pads for your own tours of security topics on the WWW.

Not only UNIX systems have vulnerabilities. Instructions for security under MS-DOS or MS Windows and Windows NT systems can be found at *http://*

www.somarsoft.com/security.htm, along with tips on correcting vulnerabilities. You should also check *http://support.microsoft.com/* for information on security topics.

The "Hacking Novell Netware FAQ," a list of vulnerabilities of various Netware versions, is located at *http://www.nmrc.org/faqs*. Every administrator of a Netware server should (have) read these!

Miscellaneous

The fingerprint of Wietse's PGP key, which you will need if you want to verify the correctness of the original SATAN sources, is

```
Type bits/keyID    Date        User ID
pub  1022/D5327CB9 1992/09/25 wietse venema <wietse@wzv.win.tue.nl>
Key fingerprint = 78 96 4A 4D F0 F0 D1 3C  45 E9 03 FC 17 67 DC D8
```

Last but not least, remember that SATAN was written to improve system security. Use it responsibly.

Index

About the Author

Martin Freiss, after a degree in electrical engineering, decided to do something else and started his working life in Unix development at Nixdorf Computer AG, writing IP stacks. As soon as he got the chance, he went into Internet administration, looking after the company's mail, news, WWW and DNS servers, protecting them from abuse and generally fiddling with everything having to do with networking on the Internet. He is currently at the Competence Center IT Networks department of Siemens Nixdorf Information Systems Inc. in Cologne, Germany, where his time is evenly divided between consulting on network security and Internet service and providing and giving seminars and workshops on these topics.

At home, he tries to improve his language skills, though—as a confessed network news addict—he spends most of his time at his workstation.

Colophon

Featured on the cover of *Protecting Networks with Satan* is a helmet from the late Medieval period. Helmets, along with body armor, have been worn as protective covering in battle since ancient times. Early armor was made of wood, leather, shells, and basketry. These materials were replaced by the far more effective metal armor early in history. In many societies, armor was a symbol of social status. With time, the armor became increasingly elaborate, as exemplified by the helmet depicted on the cover of this book. As warfare became more sopisticated and mobile, the heavy and cumbersome metal armor and helmet fell out of use.

Edie Freedman designed the cover of this book, using a 19th-century engraving from the Dover Pictorial Archive. The cover layout was produced with Quark XPress 3.3 using the ITC Garamond font. Whenever possible, our books use RepKover™, a durable and flexible lay-flat binding. If the page count exceeds RepKover's limit, perfect binding is used.

The inside layout was designed by Nancy Priest and implemented in FrameMaker by Mike Sierra. The text and heading fonts are ITC Garamond Light and Garamond Book. The illustrations that appear in the book were created in Macromedia Freehand 7.0 and screen shots were created in Adobe Photoshop 4.0 by Robert Romano. This colophon was written by Clairemarie Fisher O'Leary.

More Titles from O'Reilly

Security

Web Security & Commerce

By Simson Garfinkel with Gene Spafford
1st Edition June 1997
506 pages, ISBN 1-56592-269-7

Learn how to minimize the risks of the Web with this comprehensive guide. It covers browser vulnerabilities, privacy concerns, issues with Java, JavaScript, ActiveX, and plug-ins, digital certificates, cryptography, web server security, blocking software, censorship technology, and relevant civil and criminal issues.

Practical UNIX & Internet Security, 2nd Edition

By Simson Garfinkel & Gene Spafford
2nd Edition April 1996
1004 pages, ISBN 1-56592-148-8

This second edition of the classic *Practical UNIX Security* is a complete rewrite of the original book. It's packed with twice the pages and offers even more practical information for UNIX users and administrators. In it you'll find coverage of features of many types of UNIX systems, including SunOS, Solaris, BSDI, AIX, HP-UX, Digital UNIX, Linux, and others. Contents include UNIX and security basics, system administrator tasks, network security, and appendices containing checklists and helpful summaries.

Building Internet Firewalls

By D. Brent Chapman &
Elizabeth D. Zwicky
1st Edition September 1995
546 pages, ISBN 1-56592-124-0

Everyone is jumping on the Internet bandwagon, despite the fact that the security risks associated with connecting to the Net have never been greater. This book is a practical guide to building firewalls on the Internet. It describes a variety of firewall approaches and architectures and discusses how you can build packet filtering and proxying solutions at your site. It also contains a full discussion of how to configure Internet services (e.g., FTP, SMTP, Telnet) to work with a firewall, aswell as a complete list of resources, including the location of many publicly available firewall onstruction tools.

PGP: Pretty Good Privacy

By Simson Garfinkel
1st Edition January 1995
430 pages, ISBN 1-56592-098-8

PGP is a freely available encryption program that protects theprivacy of files and electronic mail. It uses powerful public key cryptography and works on virtually every platform. This book is both a readable technical user's guide and a fascinating behind-the-scenes look at cryptography and privacy. It describes how to use PGP and provides background on cryptography, PGP's history, battles over public key cryptography patents and U.S. government export restrictions, and publicdebates about privacy and free speech.

Computer Crime

By David Icove, Karl Seger &
William VonStorch
(Consulting Editor Eugene H. Spafford)
1st Edition August 1995
462 pages, ISBN 1-56592-086-4

This book is for anyone who needs to know what today's computer crimes look like, how to prevent them, and how to detect, investigate, and prosecute them if they do occur. It contains basic computer security information as well as guidelines for investigators, law enforcement, and system administrators. Also includes computer-related statutes and laws, a resource summary, detailed papers on computer crime, and a sample search warrant.

Computer Security Basics

By Deborah Russell & G.T. Gangemi, Sr.
1st Edition July 1991
464 pages, ISBN 0-937175-71-4

Computer Security Basics provides a broad introduction to the many areas of computer security and a detailed description of current security standards. This handbook describes complicated concepts like trusted systems,encryption, and mandatory access control in simple terms, and contains a thorough, readable introduction to the "Orange Book."

Network Administration

Using & Managing PPP

By Andrew Sun
1st Edition December 1998 (est.)
436 pages (est.), ISBN 1-56592-321-9

This book is for network administrators and others who have to set up computer systems to use PPP. It covers all aspects of the protocol, including how to set up dial-in servers, authentication, debugging, and PPP options. In addition, it contains overviews of related areas,like serial communications, DNS setup, and routing.

Managing IP Networks with Cisco Routers

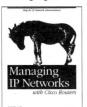

By Scott M. Ballew
1st Edition October 1997
352 pages, ISBN 1-56592-320-0

This practical guide to setting up and maintaining a production networr covers how to select routing protocols, configure protocols to handle most common situations, evaluate network equipment and vendors, and setup a help desk. Although it focuses on Cisco routers, and gives examples using Cisco's IOS, the principles discussed are common to all IP networks.

Virtual Private Networks

By Charlie Scott, Paul Wolfe & Mike Erwin
1st Edition February 1998
184 pages, ISBN 1-56592-319-7

This book tells you how to plan and build a Virtual Private Network (VPN), a collection of technologies that creates secure connections or "tunnels" over regular Internet lines. It starts with general concerns like costs and configuration and continues with detailed descriptions of how to install and use VPN technologies that are available for Windows NT and UNIX, such as PPTP and L2TP, the AltaVista Tunnel, and the Cisco PIX Firewall.

sendmail, 2nd Edition

By Bryan Costales & Eric Allman
2nd Edition January 1997
1050 pages, ISBN 1-56592-222-0

sendmail, 2nd Edition, covers sendmail Version 8.8 from Berkeley and the standard versions available on most systems. This cross-referenced edition offers an expanded tutorial, solution-oriented examples, and new topics such as the #error delivery agent, sendmail's exit values, MIME headers, and how to set up and use the user database, *mailertable*, and *smrsh*.

sendmail Desktop Reference

By Bryan Costales & Eric Allman
1st Edition March 1997
74 pages, ISBN 1-56592-278-6

This quick-reference guide provides a complete overview of the latest version of sendmail (V8.8), from command-line switches to configuration commands, from options declarations to macro definitions, and from m4 features to debugging switches—all packed into a convenient, carry-around booklet co-authored by the creator of sendmail. Includes extensive cross-references to *sendmail, Second Edition*.

Networking Personal Computers with TCP/IP

By Craig Hunt
1st Edition July 1995
408 pages, ISBN 1-56592-123-2

This book offers practical information as well as detailed instructions for attaching PCs to a TCP/IP network and its UNIX servers. It discusses the challenges you'll face and offers general advice on how to deal with them, provides basic TCP/IP configuration information for some of the popular PC operating systems, covers advanced configuration topics and configuration of specific applications such as email, and includes a chapter on on integrating Netware with TCP/IP.

Network Administration

DNS and BIND, 2nd Edition

By Paul Albitz & Cricket Liu
2nd Edition December 1996
438 pages, ISBN 1-56592-236-0

This book is a complete guide to the Internet's Domain Name System (DNS) and the Berkeley Internet Name Domain (BIND) software, the UNIX implementation of DNS. This second edition covers BIND 4.8.3, which is included in most vendor implementations today, as well as BIND 4.9.4, the potential future standard.

Getting Connected: The Internet at 56K and Up

By Kevin Dowd
1st Edition June 1996
424 pages, ISBN 1-56592-154-2

A complete guide for businesses, schools, and other organizations who want to connect their computers to the Internet. This book covers everything you need to know to make informed decisions, from helping you figure out which services you really need to providing down-to-earth explanations and configuration instructions for telecommunication options at higher than modem speeds, such as frame relay, ISDN, and leased lines. Once you're online, it shows you how to set up basic Internet services, such as a World Wide Web server. Tackles issues for PC, Macintosh, and UNIX platforms.

TCP/IP Network Administration, 2nd Edition

By Craig Hunt
2nd Edition December 1997
630 pages, ISBN 1-56592-322-7

A complete guide to setting up and running a TCP/IP network for practicing system administrators. Beyond basic setup, this new second edition discusses the Internet routing protocols and provides a tutorial on how to configure important network services. It now also includes Linux in addition to BSD and System V TCP/IP implementations.

Linux

Linux Network Administrator's Guide

By Olaf Kirch
1st Edition January 1995
370 pages, ISBN 1-56592-087-2

One of the most successful books to come from the Linux Documentation Project is the *Linux Network Administrator's Guide*. It touches on all the essential networking software included with Linux, plus some hardware considerations. Topics include serial connections, UUCP, routing and DNS, mail and News, SLIP and PPP, NFS, and NIS.

Linux Device Drivers

By Alessandro Rubini
1st Edition February 1998
432 pages, ISBN 1-56592-292-1

Linux Device Drivers is for anyone who wants to support computer peripherals under the Linux operating system or who wants to develop new hardware and run it under Linux. This practical guide shows how to write a driver for a wide range of devices, revealing information previously passed by word-of-mouth or in cryptic source code comments.

Learning the bash Shell, 2nd Edition

By Cameron Newham & Bill Rosenblatt
2nd Edition January 1998
336 pages, ISBN 1-56592-347-2

This second edition covers all of the features of *bash* Version 2.0, while still applying to *bash* Version 1.x. It includes one-dimensional arrays, parameter expansion, more pattern-matching operations, new commands, security improvements, additions to ReadLine, improved configuration and installation, and an additional programming aid, the *bash* shell debugger.

Linux

Linux in a Nutshell

By Jessica P. Hekman &
the Staff of O'Reilly & Associates
1st Edition January 1997
438 pages, ISBN 1-56592-167-4

Linux in a Nutshell covers the core
commands available on common Linux
distributions. This isn't a scaled-down
quick reference of common commands,
but a complete reference containing all user,
programming, administration, and networking commands. Also
documents a wide range of GNU tools.

Linux Multimedia Guide

By Jeff Tranter
1st Edition September 1996
386 pages, ISBN 1-56592-219-0

Linux is increasingly popular among
computer enthusiasts of all types, and one
of the applications where it is flourishing is
multimedia. This book tells you how to
program such popular devices as sound
cards, CD-ROMs, and joysticks. It also
describes the best free software packages that support manipulation
of graphics, audio, and video and offers guidance on fitting the
pieces together.

Running Linux, 2nd Edition

By Matt Welsh & Lar Kaufman
2nd Edition August 1996
650 pages, ISBN 1-56592-151-8

Linux is the most exciting development today
in the UNIX world—and some would say in
the world of the PC-compatible. A complete,
UNIX-compatible operating system developed by volunteers on the Internet, Linux is
distributed freely in electronic form and for
low cost from many vendors. This second edition of *Running Linux*
covers everything you need to understand, install, and start using
your Linux system, including a comprehensive installation tutorial,
complete information on system maintenance, tools for document
development and programming, and guidelines for network and
web site administration.

How to stay in touch with O'Reilly

1. Visit Our Award-Winning Web Site
http://www.oreilly.com/

★ "Top 100 Sites on the Web" —*PC Magazine*
★ "Top 5% Web sites" —*Point Communications*
★ "3-Star site" —*The McKinley Group*

Our web site contains a library of comprehensiveproduct information (including book excerpts and tables of contents), downloadable software, background articles, interviews with technology leaders, links to relevant sites, book cover art, and more. File us in your Bookmarks or Hotlist!

2. Join Our Email Mailing Lists
New Product Releases
To receive automatic email with brief descriptions of all new O'Reilly products as they are released, send email to:
listproc@online.oreilly.com
Put the following information in the first line of your message (*not* in the Subject field):
subscribe oreilly-news

O'Reilly Events
If you'd also like us to send information about trade show events, special promotions, and other O'Reilly events, send email to:
listproc@online.oreilly.com
Put the following information in the first line of your message (*not* in the Subject field):
subscribe oreilly-events

3. Get Examples from Our Books via FTP
There are two ways to access an archive of example files from our books:

Regular FTP
* ftp to:
  ftp.oreilly.com
  (login: anonymous
  password: your email address)
* Point your web browser to:
  ftp://ftp.oreilly.com/

FTPMAIL
* Send an email message to:
  ftpmail@online.oreilly.com
  (Write "help" in the message body)

4. Contact Us via Email
order@oreilly.com
To place a book or software order online. Good for North American and international customers.

subscriptions@oreilly.com
To place an order for any of our newsletters or periodicals.

books@oreilly.com
General questions about any of our books.

software@oreilly.com
For general questions and product information about our software. Check out O'Reilly Software Online at **http://software.oreilly.com/** for software and technical support information. Registered O'Reilly software users send your questions to: **website-support@oreilly.com**

cs@oreilly.com
For answers to problems regarding your order or our products.

booktech@oreilly.com
For book content technical questions or corrections.

proposals@oreilly.com
To submit new book or software proposals to our editors and product managers.

international@oreilly.com
For information about our international distributors or translation queries. For a list of our distributors outside of North America check out:
http://www.oreilly.com/www/order/country.html

O'Reilly & Associates, Inc.
101 Morris Street, Sebastopol, CA 95472 USA
TEL   707-829-0515 or 800-998-9938
          (6am to 5pm PST)
FAX   707-829-0104

O'REILLY™

TO ORDER: **800-998-9938** • **order@oreilly.com** • **http://www.oreilly.com/**
OUR PRODUCTS ARE AVAILABLE AT A BOOKSTORE OR SOFTWARE STORE NEAR YOU.
FOR INFORMATION: **800-998-9938** • **707-829-0515** • **info@oreilly.com**

Titles from O'Reilly

International Distributors

UK, EUROPE, MIDDLE EAST AND NORTHERN AFRICA (EXCEPT FRANCE, GERMANY, SWITZERLAND, & AUSTRIA)

INQUIRIES

International Thomson Publishing Europe
Berkshire House
168-173 High Holborn
London WC1V 7AA
United Kingdom
Telephone: 44-171-497-1422
Fax: 44-171-497-1426
Email: itpint@itps.co.uk

ORDERS

International Thomson Publishing Services, Ltd.
Cheriton House, North Way
Andover, Hampshire SP10 5BE
United Kingdom
Telephone: 44-264-342-832 (UK)
Telephone: 44-264-342-806 (outside UK)
Fax: 44-264-364418 (UK)
Fax: 44-264-342761 (outside UK)
UK & Eire orders: itpuk@itps.co.uk
International orders: itpint@itps.co.uk

FRANCE

Editions Eyrolles
61 bd Saint-Germain
75240 Paris Cedex 05
France
Fax: 33-01-44-41-11-44

FRENCH LANGUAGE BOOKS

All countries except Canada
Telephone: 33-01-44-41-46-16
Email: geodif@eyrolles.com
English language books
Telephone: 33-01-44-41-11-87
Email: distribution@eyrolles.com

GERMANY, SWITZERLAND, AND AUSTRIA

INQUIRIES

O'Reilly Verlag
Balthasarstr. 81
D-50670 Köln
Germany
Telephone: 49-221-97-31-60-0
Fax: 49-221-97-31-60-8
Email: anfragen@oreilly.de

ORDERS

International Thomson Publishing
Königswinterer Straße 418
53227 Bonn, Germany
Telephone: 49-228-97024 0
Fax: 49-228-441342
Email: order@oreilly.de

JAPAN

O'Reilly Japan, Inc.
Kiyoshige Building 2F
12-Banchi, Sanei-cho
Shinjuku-ku
Tokyo 160-0008 Japan
Telephone: 81-3-3356-5227
Fax: 81-3-3356-5261
Email: kenji@oreilly.com

INDIA

Computer Bookshop (India) PVT. Ltd.
190 Dr. D.N. Road, Fort
Bombay 400 001 India
Telephone: 91-22-207-0989
Fax: 91-22-262-3551
Email: cbsbom@giasbm01.vsnl.net.in

HONG KONG

City Discount Subscription Service Ltd.
Unit D, 3rd Floor, Yan's Tower
27 Wong Chuk Hang Road
Aberdeen, Hong Kong
Telephone: 852-2580-3539
Fax: 852-2580-6463
Email: citydis@ppn.com.hk

KOREA

Hanbit Media, Inc.
Sonyoung Bldg. 202
Yeksam-dong 736-36
Kangnam-ku
Seoul, Korea
Telephone: 822-554-9610
Fax: 822-556-0363
Email: hant93@chollian.dacom.co.kr

SINGAPORE, MALAYSIA, AND THAILAND

Addison Wesley Longman Singapore PTE Ltd.
25 First Lok Yang Road
Singapore 629734
Telephone: 65-268-2666
Fax: 65-268-7023
Email: daniel@longman.com.sg

PHILIPPINES

Mutual Books, Inc.
429-D Shaw Boulevard
Mandaluyong City, Metro
Manila, Philippines
Telephone: 632-725-7538
Fax: 632-721-3056
Email: mbikikog@mnl.sequel.net

CHINA

Ron's DataCom Co., Ltd.
79 Dongwu Avenue
Dongxihu District
Wuhan 430040
China
Telephone: 86-27-83892568
Fax: 86-27-83222108
Email: hongfeng@public.wh.hb.cn

ALL OTHER ASIAN COUNTRIES

O'Reilly & Associates, Inc.
101 Morris Street
Sebastopol, CA 95472 USA
Telephone: 707-829-0515
Fax: 707-829-0104
Email: order@oreilly.com

AUSTRALIA

WoodsLane Pty. Ltd.
7/5 Vuko Place, Warriewood NSW 2102
P.O. Box 935
Mona Vale NSW 2103
Australia
Telephone: 61-2-9970-5111
Fax: 61-2-9970-5002
Email: info@woodslane.com.au

NEW ZEALAND

Woodslane New Zealand Ltd.
21 Cooks Street (P.O. Box 575)
Waganui, New Zealand
Telephone: 64-6-347-6543
Fax: 64-6-345-4840
Email: info@woodslane.com.au

THE AMERICAS

McGraw-Hill Interamericana Editores, S.A. de C.V.
Cedro No. 512
Col. Atlampa 06450
Mexico, D.F.
Telephone: 52-5-541-3155
Fax: 52-5-541-4913
Email: mcgraw-hill@infosel.net.mx

SOUTH AFRICA

International Thomson Publishing
South Africa
Building 18, Constantia Park
138 Sixteenth Road
P.O. Box 2459
Halfway House, 1685 South Africa
Telephone: 27-11-805-4819
Fax: 27-11-805-3648

O'REILLY™

O'REILLY™

O'Reilly & Associates, Inc.
101 Morris Street
Sebastopol, CA 95472-9902
1-800-998-9938

Visit us online at:
http://www.ora.com/
orders@ora.com

O'REILLY WOULD LIKE TO HEAR FROM YOU

Which book did this card come from?

_____

Where did you buy this book?
- ❏ Bookstore   ❏ Computer Store
- ❏ Direct from O'Reilly   ❏ Class/seminar
- ❏ Bundled with hardware/software
- ❏ Other _____

What operating system do you use?
- ❏ UNIX   ❏ Macintosh
- ❏ Windows NT   ❏ PC(Windows/DOS)
- ❏ Other _____

What is your job description?
- ❏ System Administrator   ❏ Programmer
- ❏ Network Administrator   ❏ Educator/Teacher
- ❏ Web Developer
- ❏ Other _____

❏ Please send me O'Reilly's catalog, containing a complete listing of O'Reilly books and software.

Name _____   Company/Organization _____

Address _____

City _____   State _____   Zip/Postal Code _____   Country _____

Telephone _____   Internet or other email address (specify network)

Nineteenth century wood engraving
of a bear from the O'Reilly &
Associates Nutshell Handbook®
Using & Managing UUCP.

POST CARD

BUSINESS REPLY MAIL
FIRST CLASS MAIL   PERMIT NO. 80   SEBASTOPOL, CA

Postage will be paid by addressee

O'Reilly & Associates, Inc.
101 Morris Street
Sebastopol, CA 95472-9902